Steamers to the Kyles of

Andrew Clark

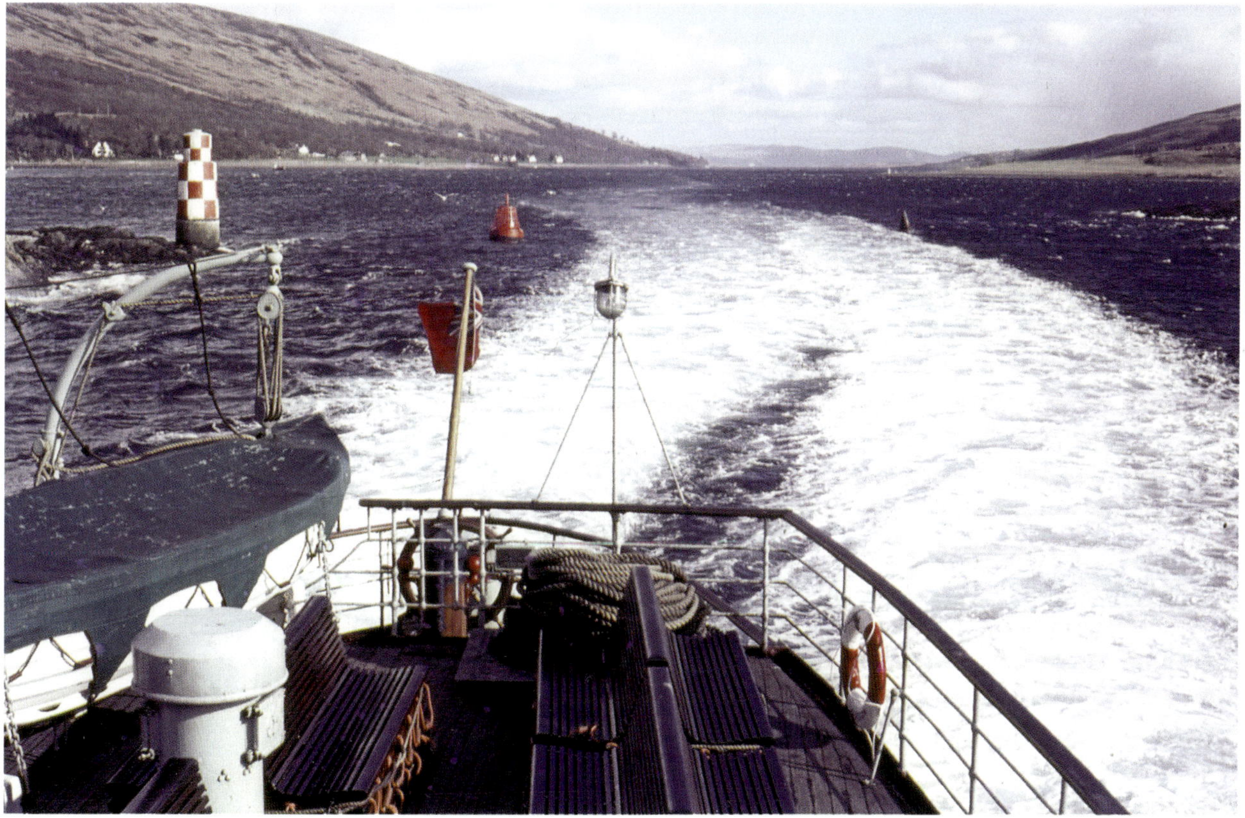

The view down the East Kyle from the Narrows on a crisp spring day in 1969, seen from the upper deck of the paddle steamer *Caledonia* in her final season.

Text © Andrew Clark, 2018.
First published in the United Kingdom, 2018,
by Stenlake Publishing Ltd.
Telephone: 01290 551122
www.stenlake.co.uk

ISBN 9781840338188

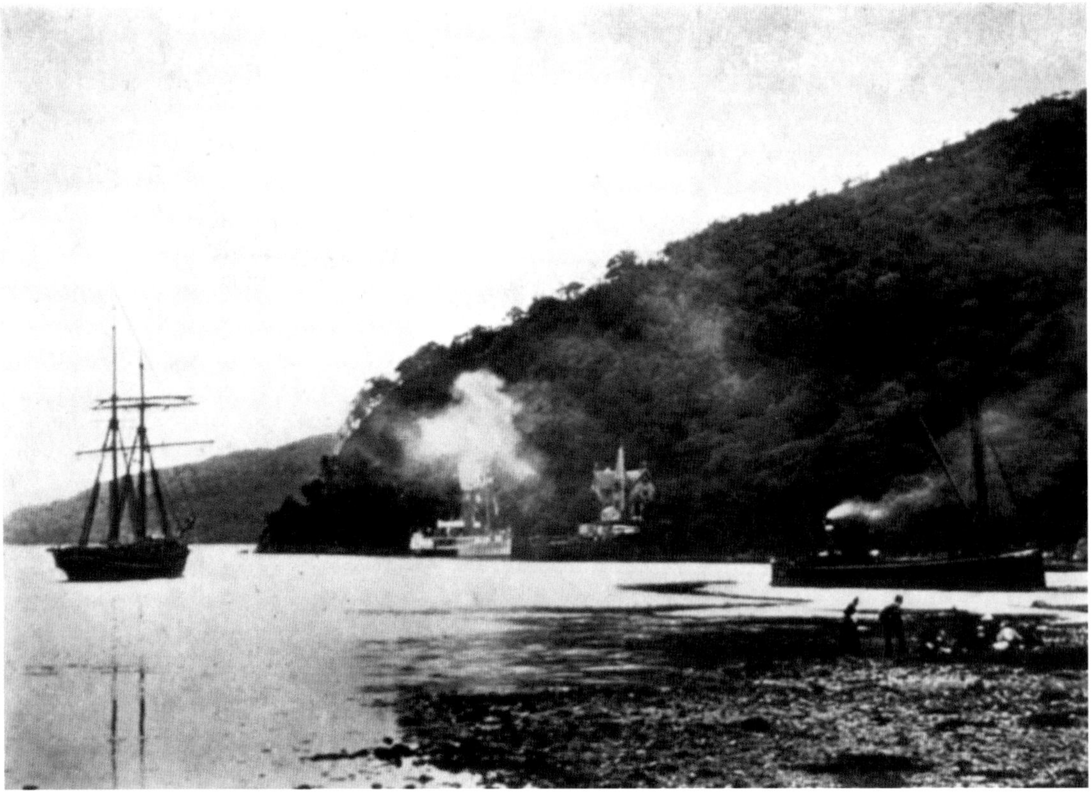

Acknowledgements

Many of the colour illustrations in this book were taken by Eric Schofield, whose photographic documentation of ships passing through the Kyles of Bute over the past 50 years is second to none. John Nicolson's painting of three paddlers near the Narrows is reproduced by courtesy of Robin Copland. Images from the Geoffrey Grimshaw Collection are published by courtesy of the McLean Museum, Inverclyde Council, and from the Tom Dunlop and Dr Joe McKendrick Collections by courtesy of the Clyde River Steamer Club. Other photos were kindly provided by A.E. Bennett, Walter Bowie, Douglas Brown, Deryk Docherty, Lawrence Macduff, Margaret Skee, the J.T.A. Brown Collection and the Estate of James Aikman Smith. Additional help came from Graeme Hogg, Graham Lappin, Iain MacLeod, John Newth and Craig Osborne.

Left: Ormidale, Loch Riddon, *circa* 1900, with the Glasgow & South Western Railway's *Minerva* at the pier, a puffer unloading on the right and holidaymakers on the shore.

Introduction

Since the earliest days of mechanically powered shipping 200 years ago, the Kyles of Bute have inspired a sense of wonder. They were "a tortuous gorge", "a great rift in the mountains", "this perplexing passage". One pre-Victorian tourist, describing his reactions barely 10 years after *Comet*'s pioneering voyage down the River Clyde in 1812, remarked that "Few scenes exist of a more romantic character than those which occur in the fairy mazes of the Kyles of Bute. At every turn all further progress seems to be denied through the intricate mixture of land and water, the steam packet all the while winding among broken rocks and woody shore, or under overhanging cliffs and loftier hills. We seemed to be threading a perfect labyrinth; and the perpetual shifting of the scenery, from the constant alteration of our course, had a novel and pleasing effect."

The tone may not quite match the exclamations of wonder on the decks of *Waverley* today as she paddles through the Narrows, but the sentiment is the same. This heather clad scenery, offering a perspective of many miles at some points and little more than a few hundred yards at others, is one of earth's glories, and you don't need to travel far from metropolitan life or pay big money to see it. It is on our doorstep, there to be discovered in the same way that captivated the early Victorians – from a ship.

Of course, many more people now experience the Kyles from the roadside than from the water but, until the second half of the 20th century, the only viable way was by sea. The Kyles through a windscreen, or from the 'new road' to Tighnabruaich, offer a fraction of the impact they create from a steamer. From the roadside you are a spectator. On the water you are a participant in an ever-evolving panorama.

As the Kyles have become more accessible by road, opportunities to experience them from the water have dwindled. Until the early 1970s pleasure steamers sailed through on a daily basis. Today, unless you have a yacht or motor boat, you are restricted to *Waverley*'s two-month summer season.

In the first half of the 19th century the Kyles were not so much a destination, more a short cut for steamers transporting passengers and cargo from Glasgow to Loch Fyne. Much of that trade was conducted by a conglomerate known as the Castle Steam Packet Company. Their vessels embarked or disembarked passengers by flit boat or at primitive jetties at the villages they passed, from Colintraive to Ardlamont. The steamer was virtually the only point of contact these communities had with the outside world. The Castle boats were superseded in 1851 by David Hutcheson and later David MacBrayne: their beautiful ships, subsidised by the Royal Mail, were the first to develop the tourist potential of the West Highlands, of which the Kyles offered the first authentic sniff.

The Kames Gunpowder Works, founded at Millhouse in 1839, were an early sign of so-called civilisation: the company had its own stone quay and, from 1849, a steamer appropriately named *Guy Fawkes*. The construction of a steamer pier at Kames in 1855 – as at Tighnabruaich, Ormidale and Colintraive soon after – was prompted by property speculation, as local lairds made a killing from what till then had been unremunerative coastal land. Feuing – the selling of ground for the construction of summer villas by wealthy Glaswegians – became all the rage. The resulting properties command some of the best views along Scotland's west coast. It was the presence of well-heeled summer commuters that spurred the railway companies and their steam packet offshoots in the 1890s to give the Kyles the kind of luxury service that, from today's perspective, seems almost unreal. Kyles communities never had it so good.

After signs of decline in the mid-to-late 20th century, the Kyles of Bute are once again a weekenders' paradise: yacht moorings and holiday houses proliferate. The realigned buoys at the Narrows may have made the passage from East to West Kyle even narrower, but the scenery remains unchanged, making a voyage through them every bit as magical as it was for passengers on the steamers pictured in these pages.

Andrew Clark
Glasgow, June 2018

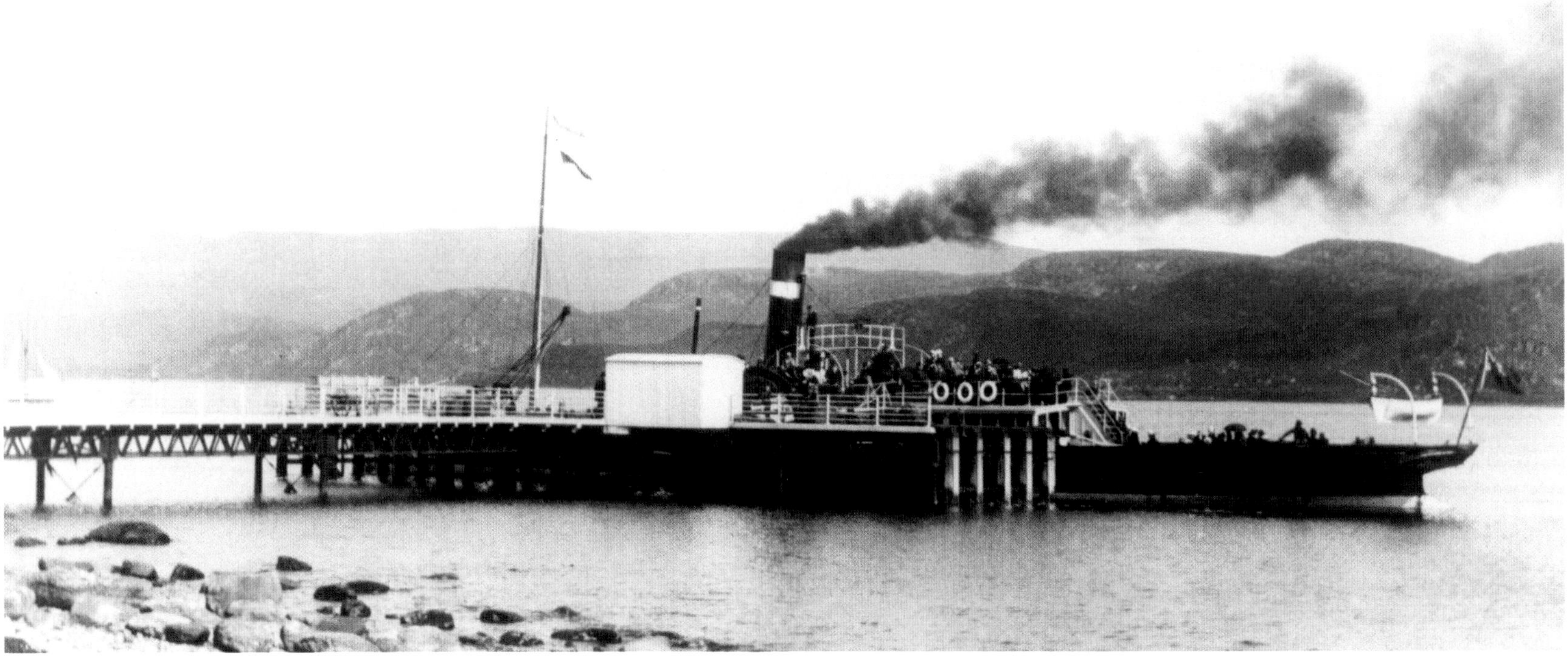

Captain McLean's *Marquis of Bute* (1868) lies at Auchenlochan Pier in the mid 1880s. Situated immediately south of Kames, Auchenlochan was the last of the Kyles villages to acquire a steamer pier. Its construction in 1879 coincided with the formation of a road from Kames to Ardlamont at the southern end of the West Kyle, continuing round to Tighnabruaich via Corra Farm and Kilbride Church: pier and road brought Auchenlochan into the modern age. The pier initiative came from the local landowner, John Malcolm of Poltalloch, who footed the £2,200 bill. Reporting on the "fine new iron pier" on Saturday 23 August 1879, the *Greenock Advertiser* gave the following description: "The new structure was executed in accordance with plans prepared by Messrs Wharrie, Colledge, Brand, civil engineers, Glasgow. The gangway is 250 feet in length from the shore to the pierhead, rests upon Warne's girders, and these are supported by cast iron columns placed 30 feet apart. The pierhead, 108 feet long by 20 feet wide, is carried upon malleable iron piles which are driven into the ground and securely fixed. On the pierhead a small wooden waiting room has been erected, while at the shore end a ladies' waiting room, ticket office and store are provided in a stone building. At low tide the depth of water at the pierhead is nine feet." The pier, which had taken the Glasgow engineering company Messrs A. & W. Smith five months to construct, was put "under the charge of Robert Duncan of the Royal Hotel, who has contracted for it." The first steamer to call was Captain Alexander Williamson's *Viceroy* of 1875.

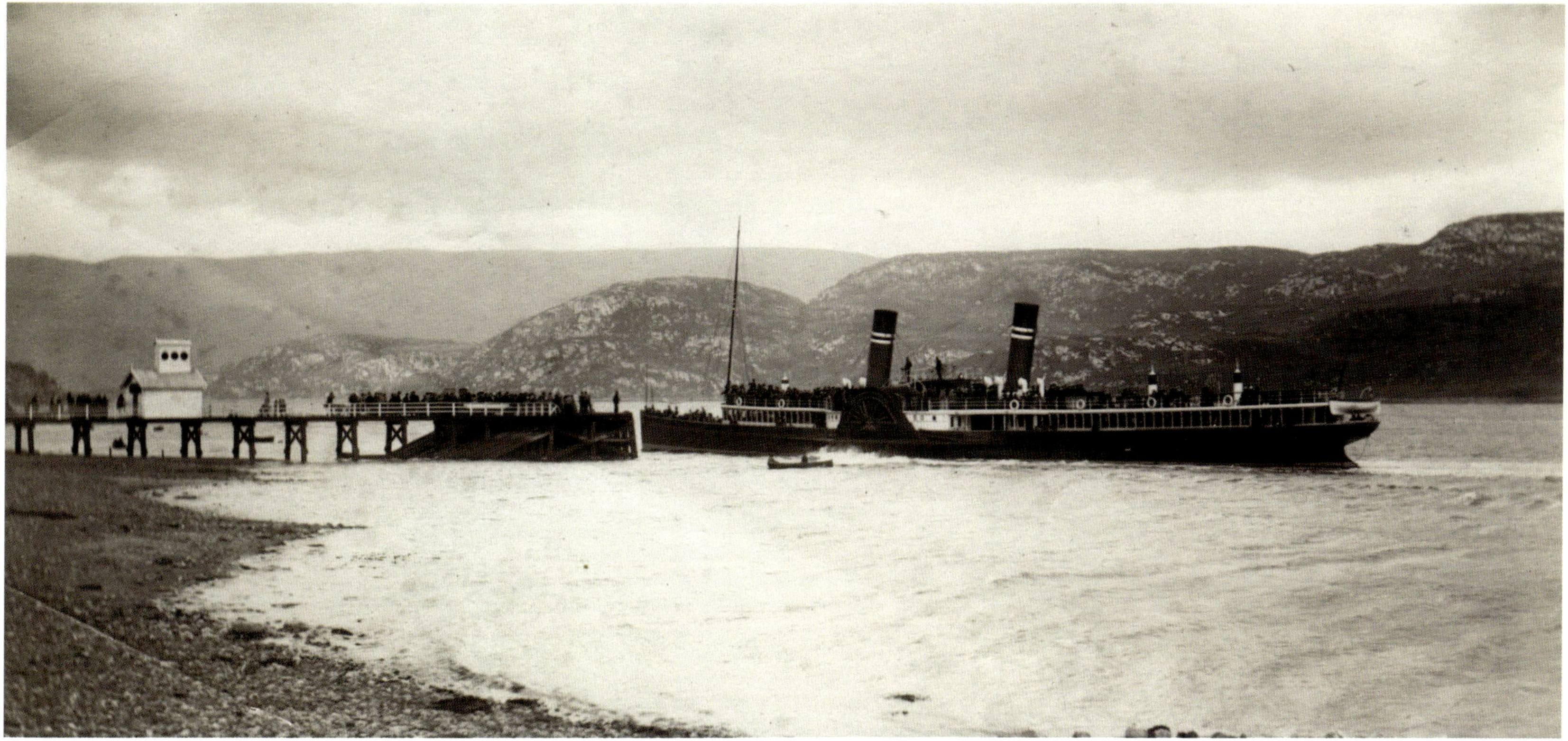

The first *Lord of the Isles* arrives at Tighnabruaich on the return journey of her daily voyage from Glasgow to Inveraray. The date is 1890 or 1891, the year before she was replaced by a bigger steamer of the same name. Until the 1850s the sheltered shoreline of the West Kyle was largely the preserve of fishermen and crofters, untroubled by wider civilisation apart from steamers passing on their way to Loch Fyne. Admiralty charts of 1849 and 1852 do not even show Tighnabruaich. Visiting steamers used the 'Innens jetty', situated where Tighnabruaich Pier stands today. The village was a mid-Victorian creation and came about as a result of the feuing of ground to wealthy Glaswegian industrialists, who constructed handsome summer residences there, prompting the inauguration of a seasonal daily service to Glasgow in 1856. A pier house was built in 1857, and by the early 1860s references to Innens had disappeared in favour of Tighnabruaich ('the house on the hill'), which thereafter ranked as the principal Kyles destination. Despite pier dues levied by Arthur Scoular, the local laird, maintenance of the structure did not keep pace with the increasing size and sophistication of the Clyde's steamers, the most important being the Hutcheson/MacBrayne flagships *Iona* (1864) and *Columba* (1878), and the Glasgow & Inveraray Steamboat Company's beautifully proportioned *Lord of the Isles* (1877). Reconstruction, begun in 1884, was completed in the spring of 1885, so this photograph shows the pier in near-pristine state. *Lord of the Isles* covered 228 miles daily in just over 12 ½ hours of steaming, including a dozen stops on her way to the head of Loch Fyne – a feat of speed and efficiency that justified her fame.

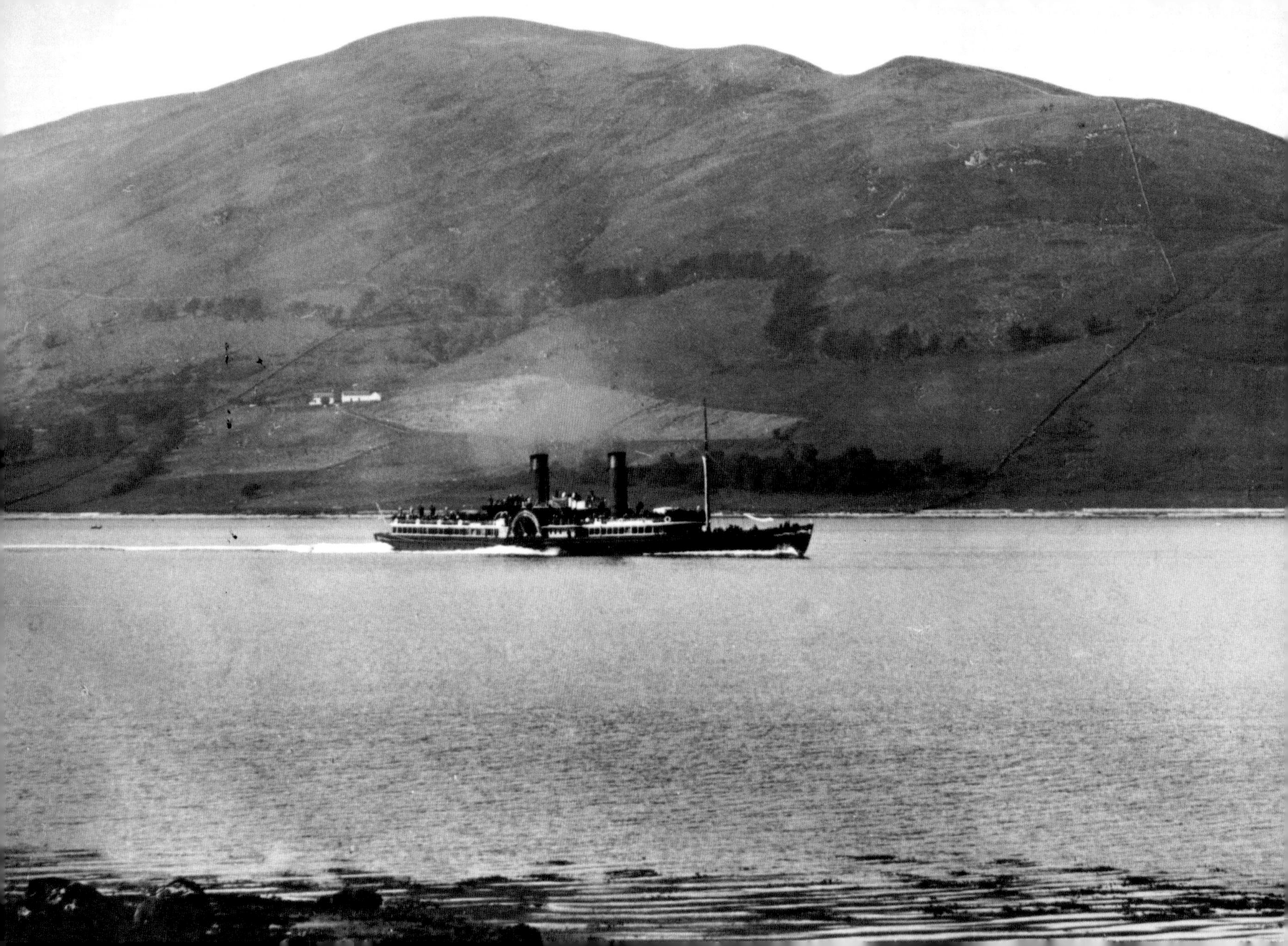

Facing page: the arrival of the sleek, swift, sophisticated *Lord of the Isles* in 1877 posed a threat to the Hutcheson/MacBrayne company's well-established Loch Fyne trade, and MacBrayne responded in 1878 with *Columba*, widely considered to be the finest coastal steamer ever built. At 301 feet she was by far the longest Clyde vessel of her day, a record superseded only in 1993 by the Arran ferry *Caledonian Isles*. Every summer until her withdrawal at the end of the 1935 season, *Columba* steamed through the Kyles of Bute twice daily, outward and return from Glasgow to Tarbert and Ardrishaig – the first leg of 'the Royal Route' to the Highlands, so named because of Queen Victoria's 1847 visit by sea to the West of Scotland. *Columba* is seen here in all her majesty, emerging from the East Kyle on the homeward run to Rothesay, Innellan, Dunoon, Gourock, Greenock and Glasgow.

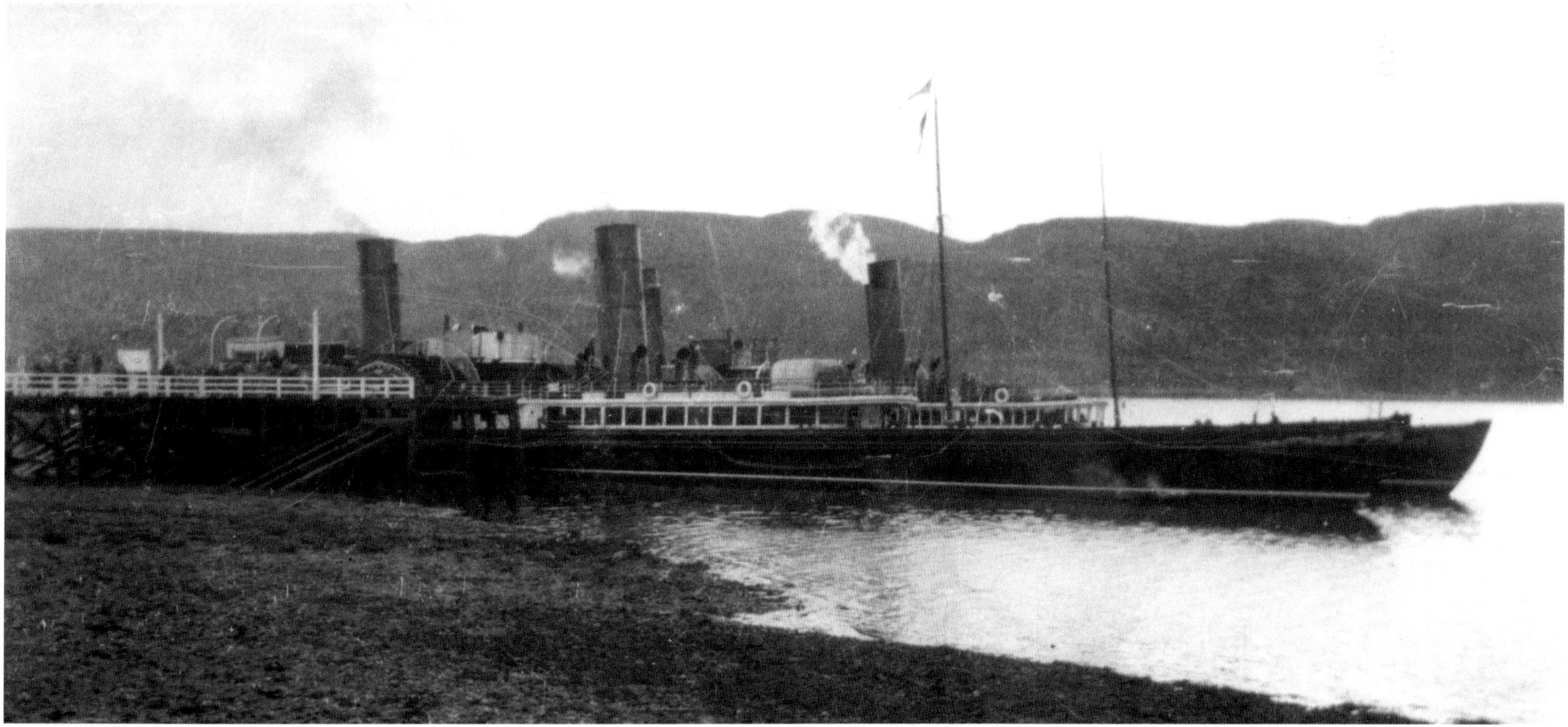

Above: *Columba* (nearest the camera) was a superior version of *Iona*, which had set new standards for tourist travel to the West Highlands when she came out in 1864. After *Columba*'s arrival *Iona* was put on a supplementary service between Ardrishaig and Glasgow, although she usually operated the main service in spring and autumn: the larger ship was in steam for little more than three months at the height of summer. The two ships had similar features – canoe-like bow, square stern and twin funnels fore and aft of cylindrical paddle-boxes – but they were never timetabled to berth simultaneously at the same pier, least of all facing the same way in the Kyles of Bute. It is not known what prompted this exceptional occasion at Tighnabruaich, dating from the late 1920s or early 1930s.

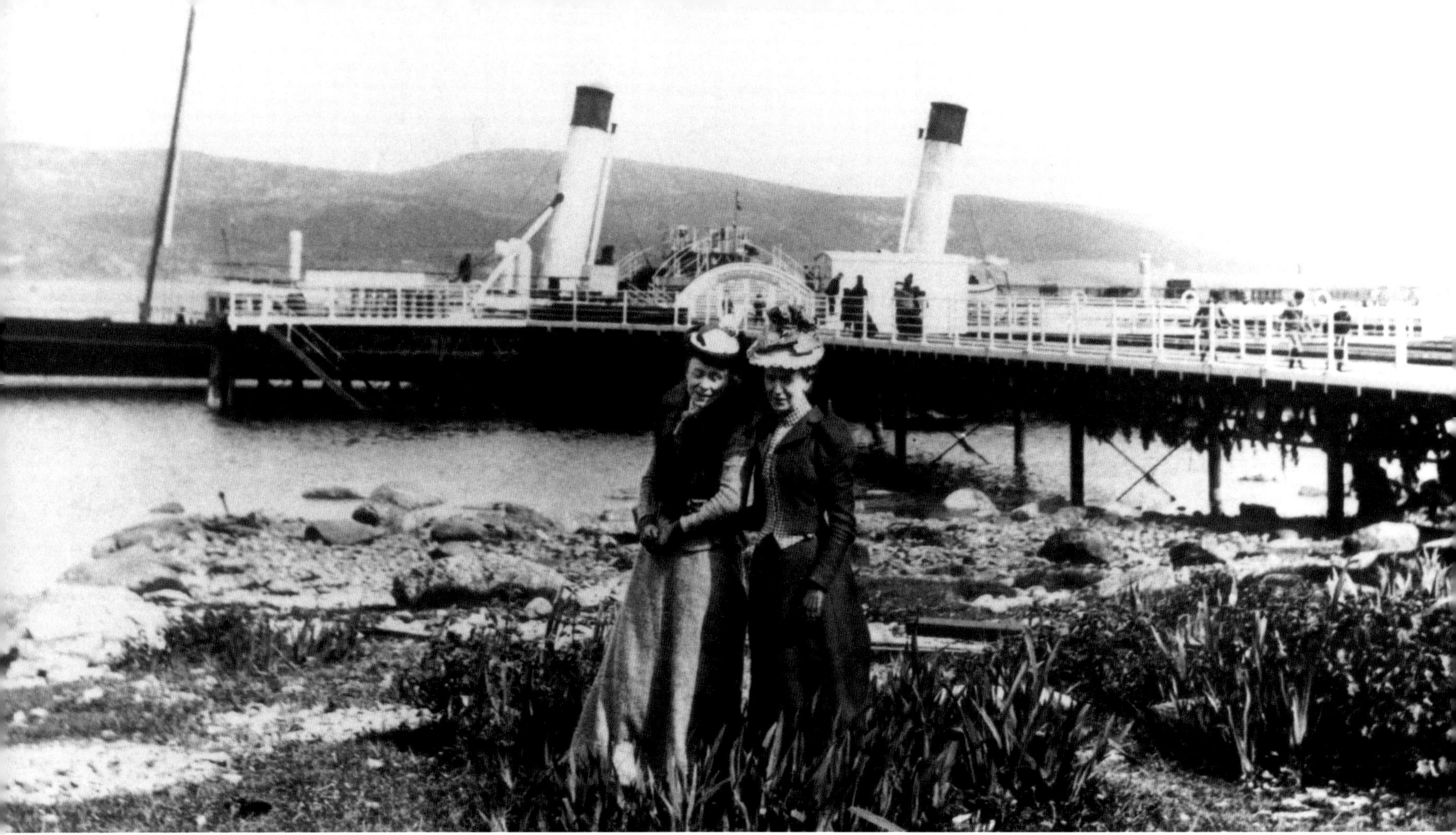

A pair of excursionists sample the delights of Auchenlochan *circa* 1890: the location is given away by the distinctive wooden shelter on the pier. The steamer is *Victoria* of 1886, the pride of Captain Alexander Campbell's Wemyss Bay fleet and the first Clyde steamer with electric light. He used her to develop his lucrative excursion trade, to the dismay of regular customers on his Wemyss Bay-Rothesay service, who had to make do with older, less comfortable boats. When the Caledonian Railway acquired the Greenock and Wemyss Bay Railway Company and established its own steamer fleet in 1889-90, Captain Campbell was forced to sell up. *Victoria* left the Clyde after the 1890 season, returning briefly in 1892-93 and 1897. While Auchenlochan served as an occasional destination for excursion steamers and cargo boats, it was bypassed by the bigger steamers heading beyond the Kyles.

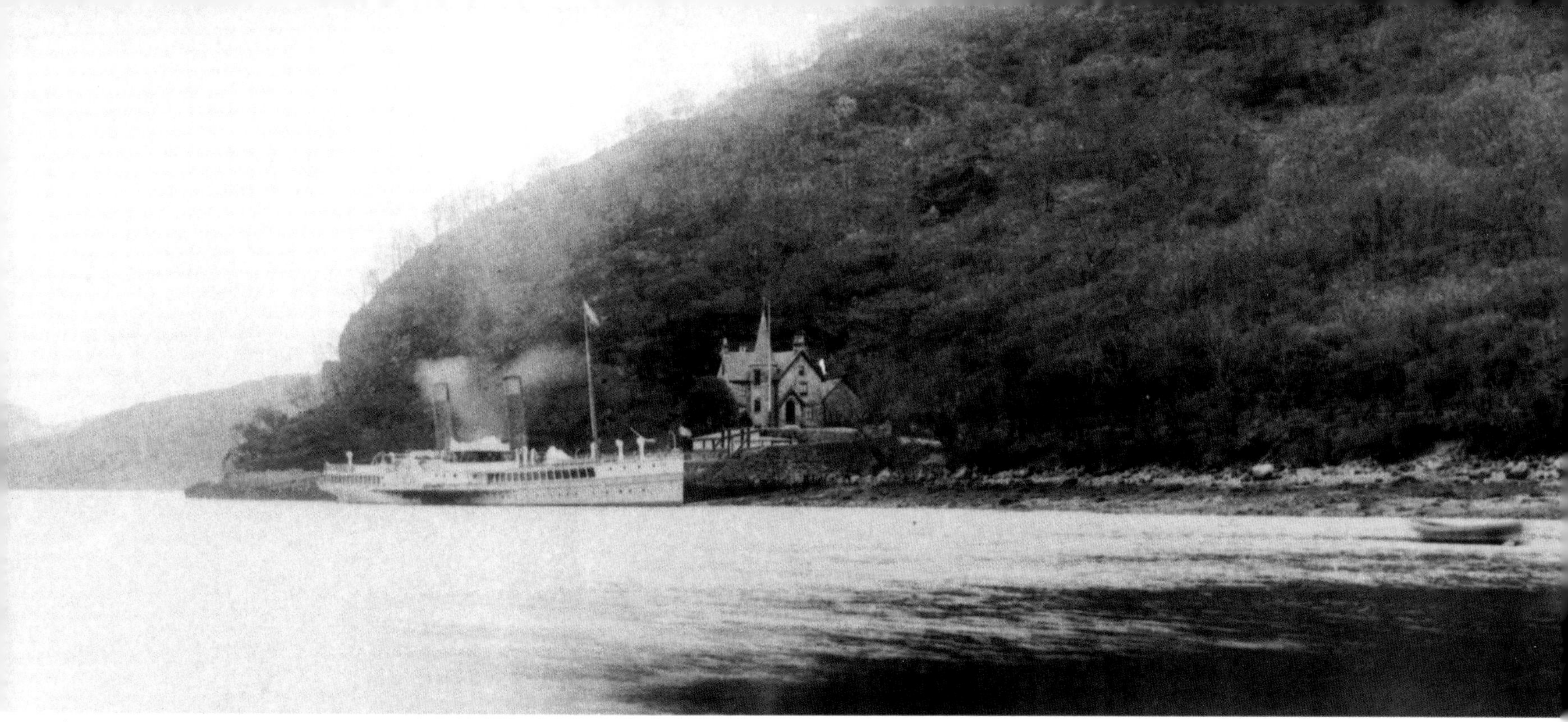

The pier at Ormidale, a remote spot along the west bank of Loch Riddon, was built in 1855 at the same time as a hotel: both were financed by the local laird, Colonel Campbell, with the expectation – never properly fulfilled – that they would stimulate feuing of ground in a manner similar to other Kyles communities. In December that year the Glasgow and Lochfyne Steam Packet Company inaugurated a weekly call by its passenger and cargo steamers *Mary Jane* and *Inveraray Castle*, and in July 1856 Ormidale was linked into a new daily commuter service from Kyles piers to Glasgow. This was inaugurated by *Sir Colin Campbell*, a curious vessel owned by Paisley shipbuilder John Barr and constructed by him the previous year with two bows – an advantage at the head of Loch Riddon, where turning space is limited. Although *Sir Colin Campbell* was sold off the Clyde later that year, her place was taken by a succession of other, more conventional steamers. From the 1860s, thanks to its cocoon-like tranquility, Ormidale also became a popular excursion destination. The vessel here is the Glasgow & South Western Railway's opulent flagship *Glen Sannox*, the dominant presence on the Ardrossan-Arran run in the pre-1914 era. Her visit to Ormidale on 8 May 1896 is believed to be the only time she called there. "This fine steamer was taken out of the harbour the other day after an extensive overhaul, in first-class trim," reported the *Greenock Telegraph* on 9 May, "and yesterday went upon an extended cruise ... The steamer, in charge of Captain Macgregor, sailed first to Arrochar, then visited Loch Goil; leaving there the Kyles of Bute were headed for and a visit paid to Ormidale. The cruise was then extended to Campbeltown Loch, thence round Ailsa and on to Fairlie, and back to Princes Pier, a most enjoyable day having been spent ... She will be placed on the Ardrossan and Arran route on Monday week."

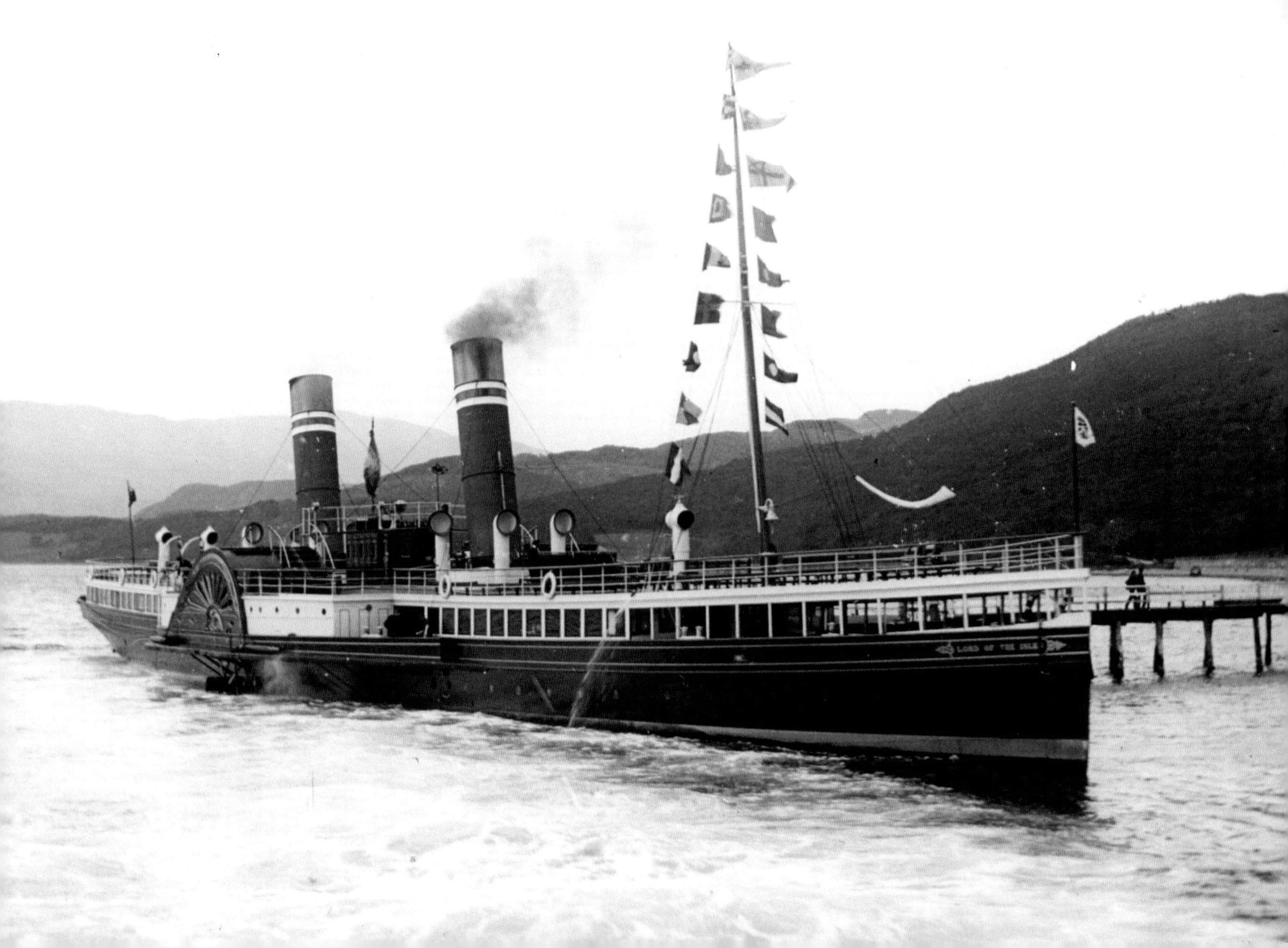

Facing page: in the pre-modern era, cattle were made to swim across a 300-yard channel on their way from the island of Bute to mainland markets. Their point of landing was Colintraive, meaning 'swimming narrows'. Its significance as a ferry point has always outshone its role as a steamer destination, but from the 1840s until 1948 it had a pier that provided a direct connection with Glasgow. Built on a spit jutting into the East Kyle and extended in 1859, the pier required minimal deviation from the route to and from the Narrows. The Hutcheson/MacBrayne mail steamer called daily on its way to and from Tarbert and Ardrishaig, but its Glasgow & Inveraray Steamboat Company rival, with further to go, had no time to stop, and generally whizzed past as *Columba* or *Iona* slowed for the call. That makes this photograph of the second *Lord of the Isles* all the more treasurable: the flags indicate she is visiting Colintraive on a special charter. Her excursion party has gone ashore. The crew have left a hose running over the side and the pier hands are leaving after casting off the ropes of another paddler (probably MacBrayne's mail steamer), from which the photo is taken.

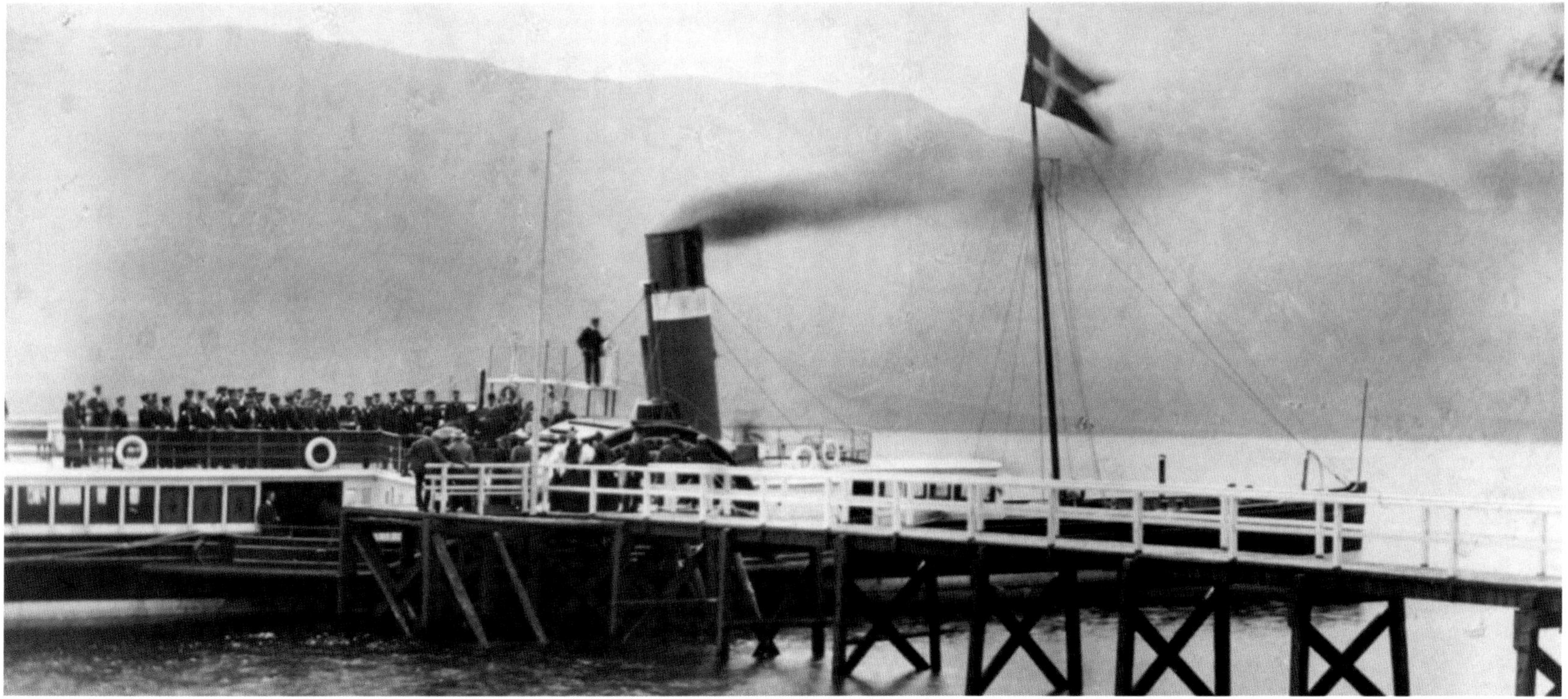

Above: Loch Striven has always been one of the Clyde's most unspoilt lochs: unlike Loch Riddon it never had a scheduled steamer service. Berry's Pier, on the eastern shore, is believed to have been built by the Berry family, the local landowners, at some point in the mid to late 19th century. This photo of a visit by the North British Railway's *Diana Vernon* dates from 13 July 1892, when Walter Berry, Danish Consul in Scotland, arranged for a party of 40 Danish naval cadets to sail from the NBR railhead at Craigendoran to his Glenstriven estate. Built in 1885, *Diana Vernon* was sold in 1901 to Brighton (operating there as *Worthing Belle*) and in 1913 to Turkey.

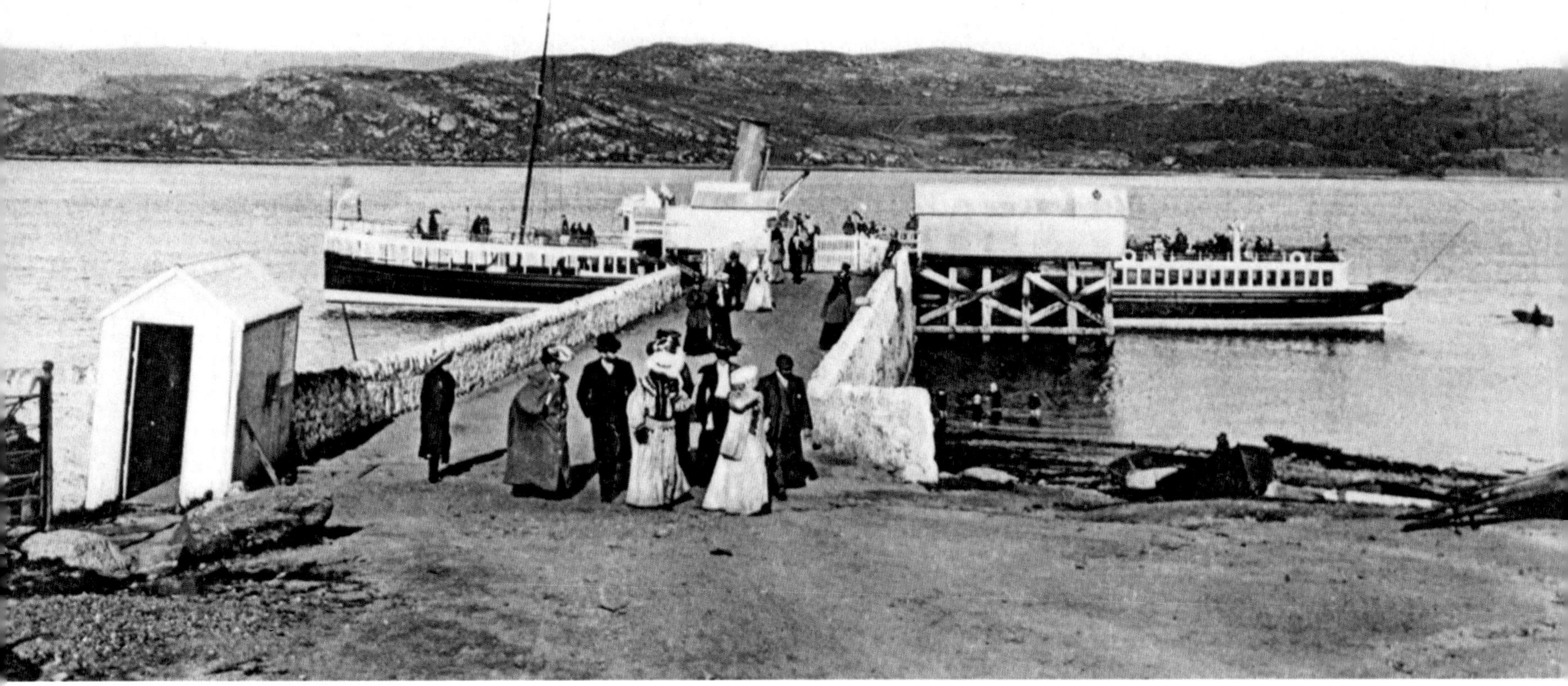

The communities around the Kyles of Bute never had it so good as in the 25 years between 1889 and 1914. This was the 'golden era' of the Clyde steamers. Pushing aside private operators in a bid to corner the coast trade, railway companies built their own fleets of high-quality, loss-making steamers, often duplicating each other's services in a competition from which no one emerged the winner – except the people in the Kyles villages, who enjoyed connections with the outside world of unparalleled style and frequency. *Marchioness of Lorne*, pictured at Kames Pier in the early years of the 20th century, is typical of that era. She was built in 1891 for the Caledonian Steam Packet Company (CSP), the steamer-operating arm of the Caledonian Railway, and like other CSP steamers of the 1890s and 1900s, her promenade deck extended right to the bow, with the foremost part not plated in to allow rope-handling on the main deck. *Marchioness of Lorne* saw First World War service at Malta, without any Scottish crewmen, but returned in such poor condition that she was not reconditioned.

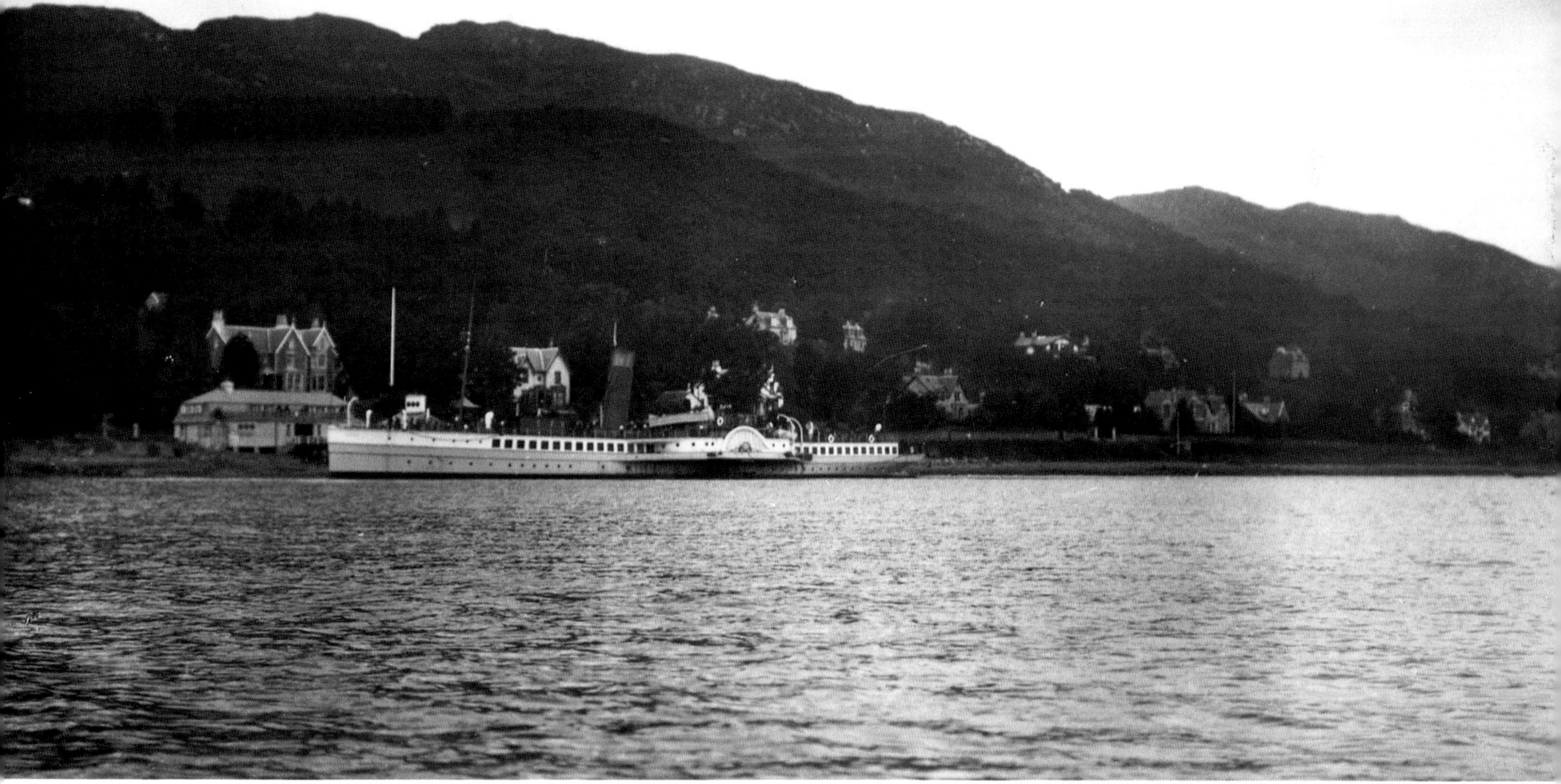

By the early 1900s Tighnabruaich was indisputably the busiest pier in the Kyles of Bute, a fixture as much for summer excursion steamers as year-round service boats: it has been estimated that in 1903 the number of daily calls there was as high as 28. As the Glasgow & South Western Railway's Ayr excursion steamer, *Juno* made occasional visits. Built in 1898, she was more heavily constructed than most Clyde contemporaries, having reputedly been ordered for south of England service and bought 'on the stocks' at Clydebank when her intended owners failed to raise the purchase price. Apart from the summer of 1919, when she was the G&SWR's Kyles boat (berthing overnight at Kames), she devoted her entire peacetime career to the Ayr excursion roster, which took her all over the Firth of Clyde, including the Kyles piers. She was withdrawn at the end of the 1931 season and broken up the following spring at Alloa.

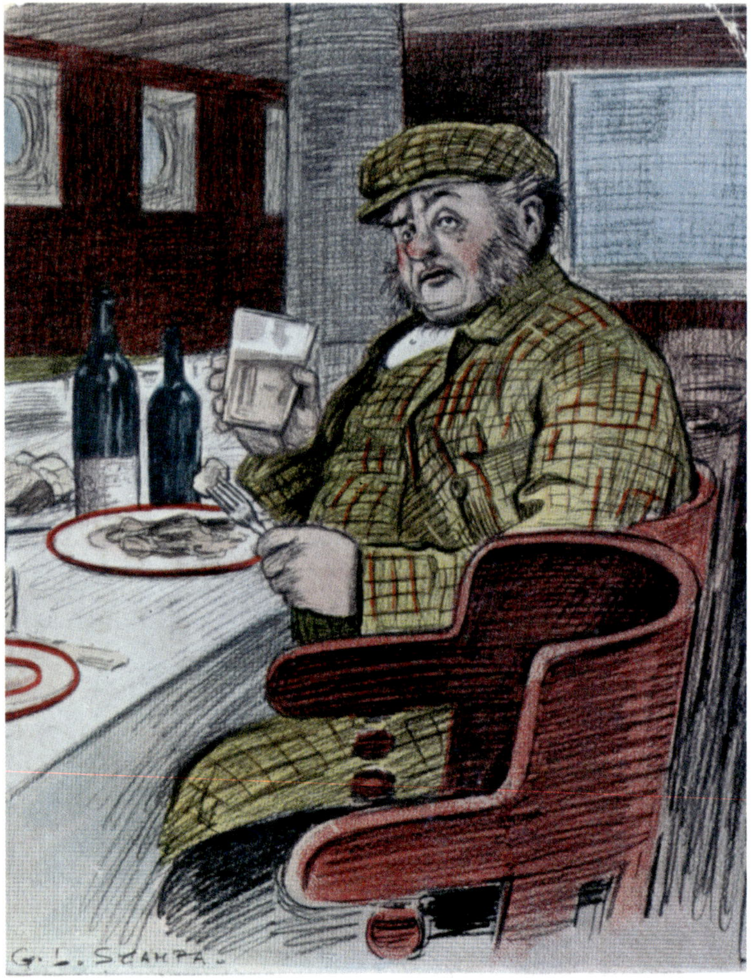

Scene: The Dining-Saloon of a Steamer on the Clyde.

Voice from above—"Come up, Jock, come up! Here's the Kyles of Bute!"

Jock—"Deil tak' the Kyles o' Bute! D'ye think I'm gaun tae spoil ma holidays wi' scenery?"

From their debut in the early 19th century, Clyde steamers were widely seen as dens of alcohol: drunken behaviour on board became so commonplace that in 1880 the temperance movement promoted the building of a pleasure steamer, *Ivanhoe*, that would operate on the teetotal principle. It was a well-meaning experiment which, on other ships, did nothing to reduce the pleasure of a visit to the bar on the lower deck – a habit which, if the head of the family was travelling with his wife and children, would invariably be passed off as father 'going down to see the engines'.

Facing page: *Mars* leaves Colintraive Pier on the G&SWR's afternoon run to Ormidale and West Kyle piers. Built in 1902 for upper-firth services, *Mars* was a purposeful little steamer that remained out of the limelight for her 15 years of Clyde service. Requisitioned by the Admiralty in September 1916 and renamed *Marsa*, she was run down by a destroyer at night off Harwich in November 1917, and broke in two during a salvage attempt. One of her captains had strong Kyles connections: Andrew Turner, Master in 1913-14, was born at Colintraive and, a year after leaving *Mars*, became piermaster at Kames.

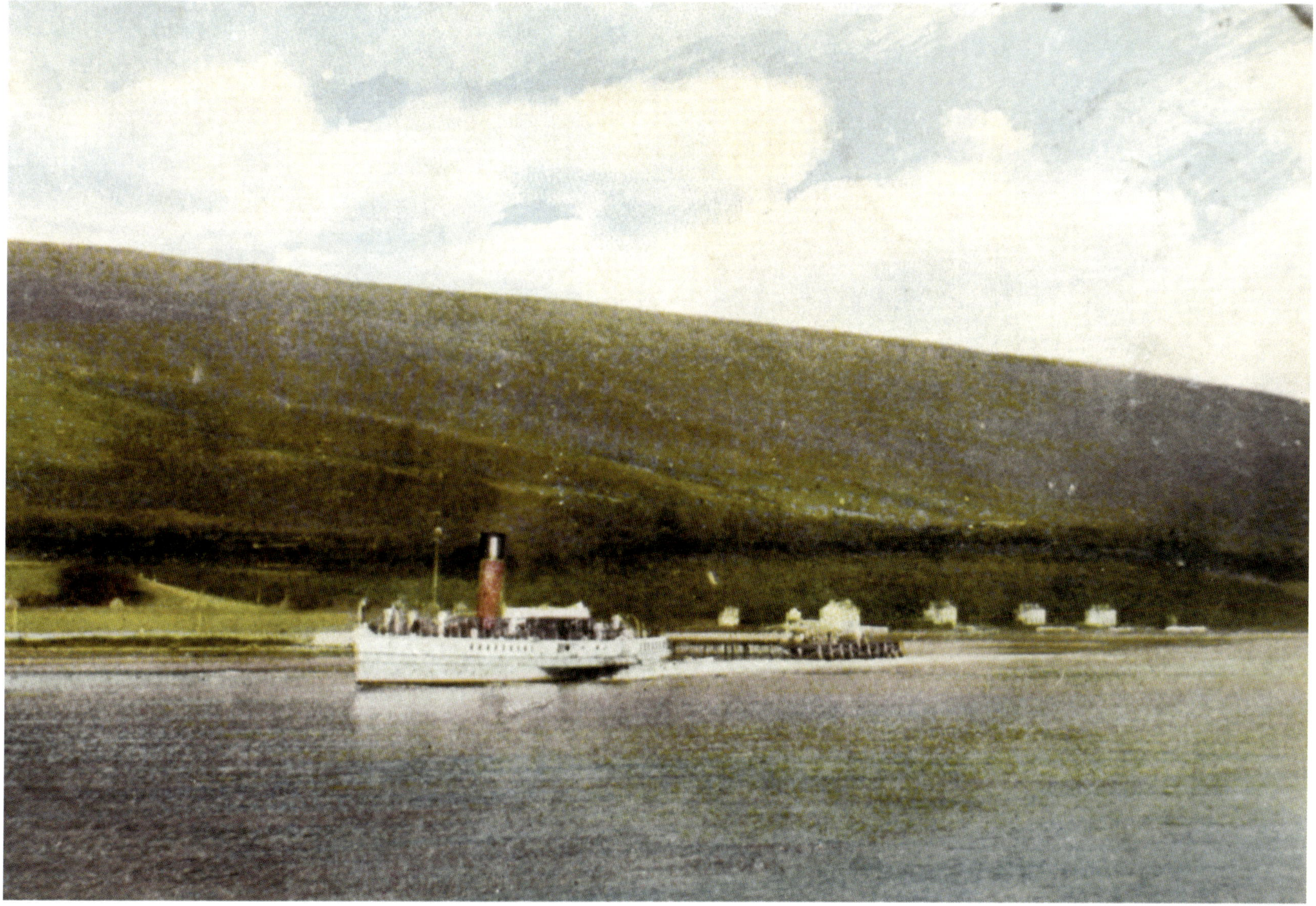

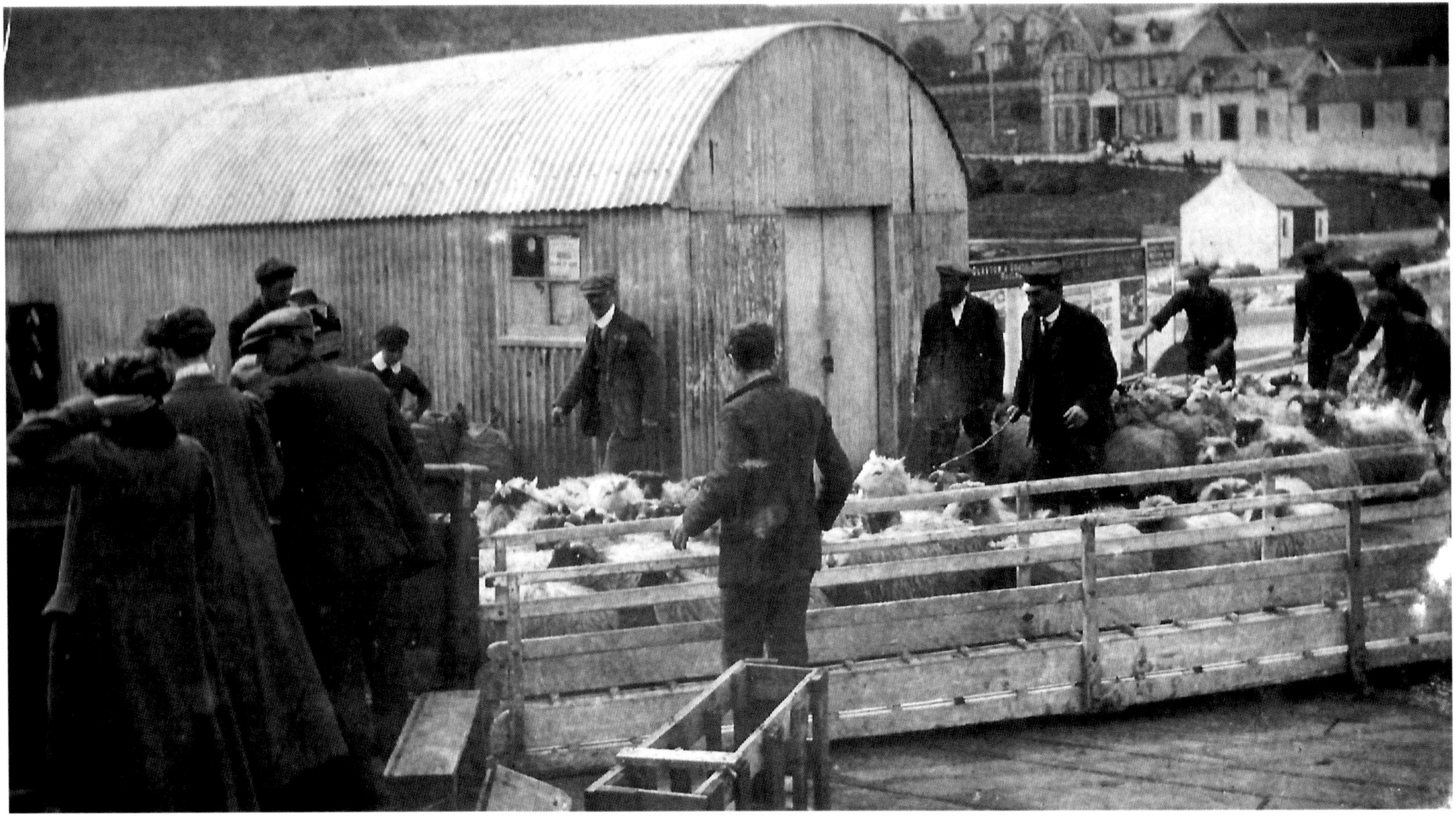

At the end of the 1928 summer Kames became the first of the Kyles communities to lose its regular steamer connection, but it did not immediately lose its pier. From the early 19th century until the advent of car ferries in the 1950s, Clyde piers were not only an arrival or departure point for well-heeled commuters and genteel excursionists. They fulfilled an equally important, albeit less glamorous, role as the transfer point for livestock being sent to market from islands and other isolated communities. This scene at Kames predates the 1914-18 war and shows sheep being herded towards the pier-end for loading onto *Cygnet*, a propeller-driven vessel owned by David MacBrayne Ltd. Initially used for cargo and cattle runs on the Clyde, *Cygnet* moved to the company's West Highland routes for the latter part of the 1914-18 war. She served on the Oban-Lochboisdale run in the 1920s, with part of her accommodation modestly adapted for passengers – many of whom complained loudly that they were being treated like cattle.

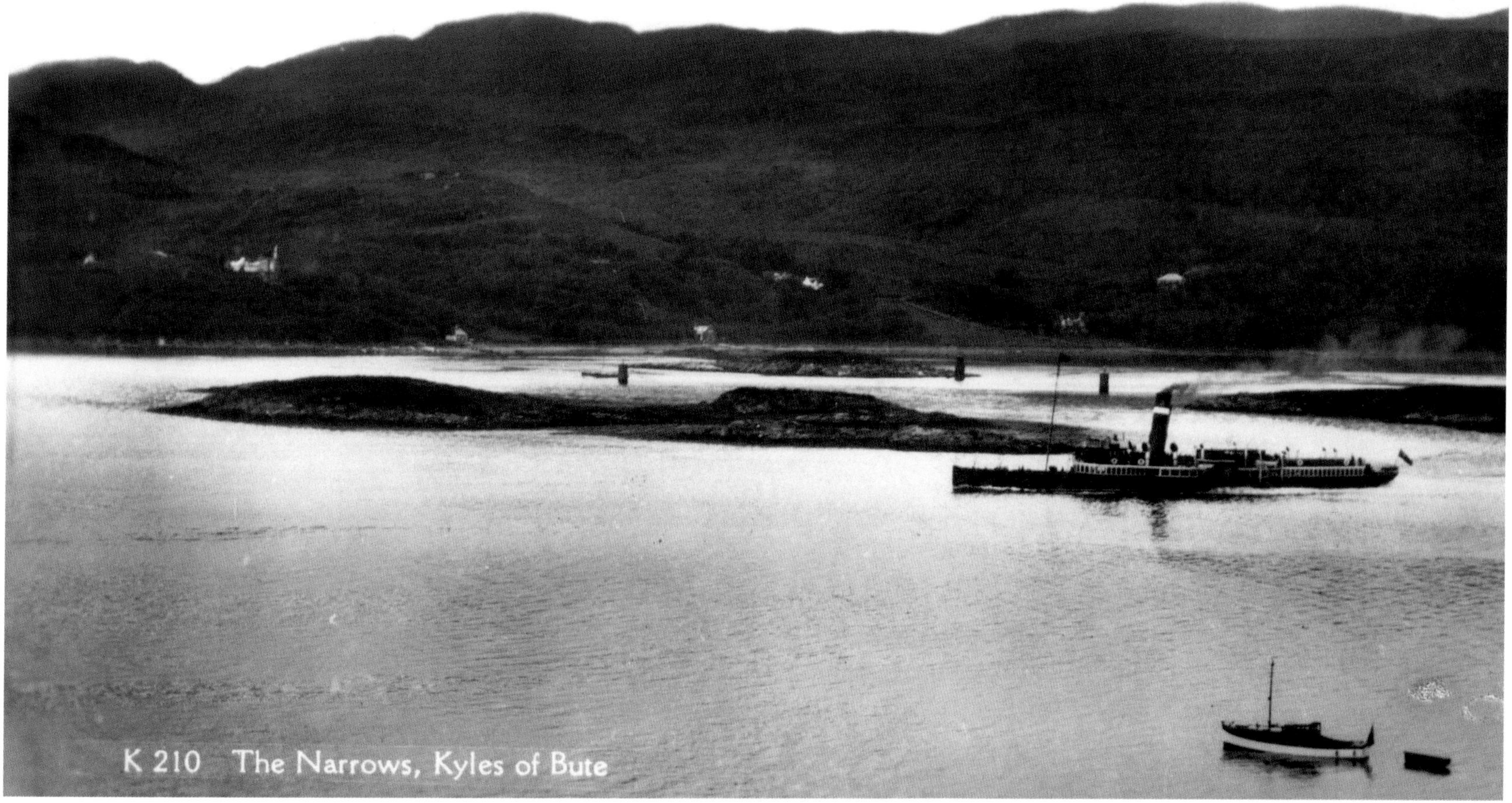

Steaming through the Narrows at the Kyles of Bute has long ranked as one of the most thrilling experiences around Britain's coastline: the ship's speed drops as the landscape apparently blocking the way opens up to reveal a passage just wide enough to squeeze through. With rocky islands on either side that seem almost within touching distance, the ship steers a straight course between well-marked buoys – a scene captured in a multitude of picture postcards from the late 19th century onwards. What this postcard documents is a much rarer occurrence – a steamer (either *Talisman* or *Kenilworth*) taking the dogleg route on the southern side of the Narrows. Wider but also shallower and riskier than the main channel, the dogleg was a viable alternative for shallow-draughted paddle steamers, especially when another vessel was coming through the main channel in the opposite direction. When the tide is right, it remains an option for *Waverley*, the Clyde's last steamer.

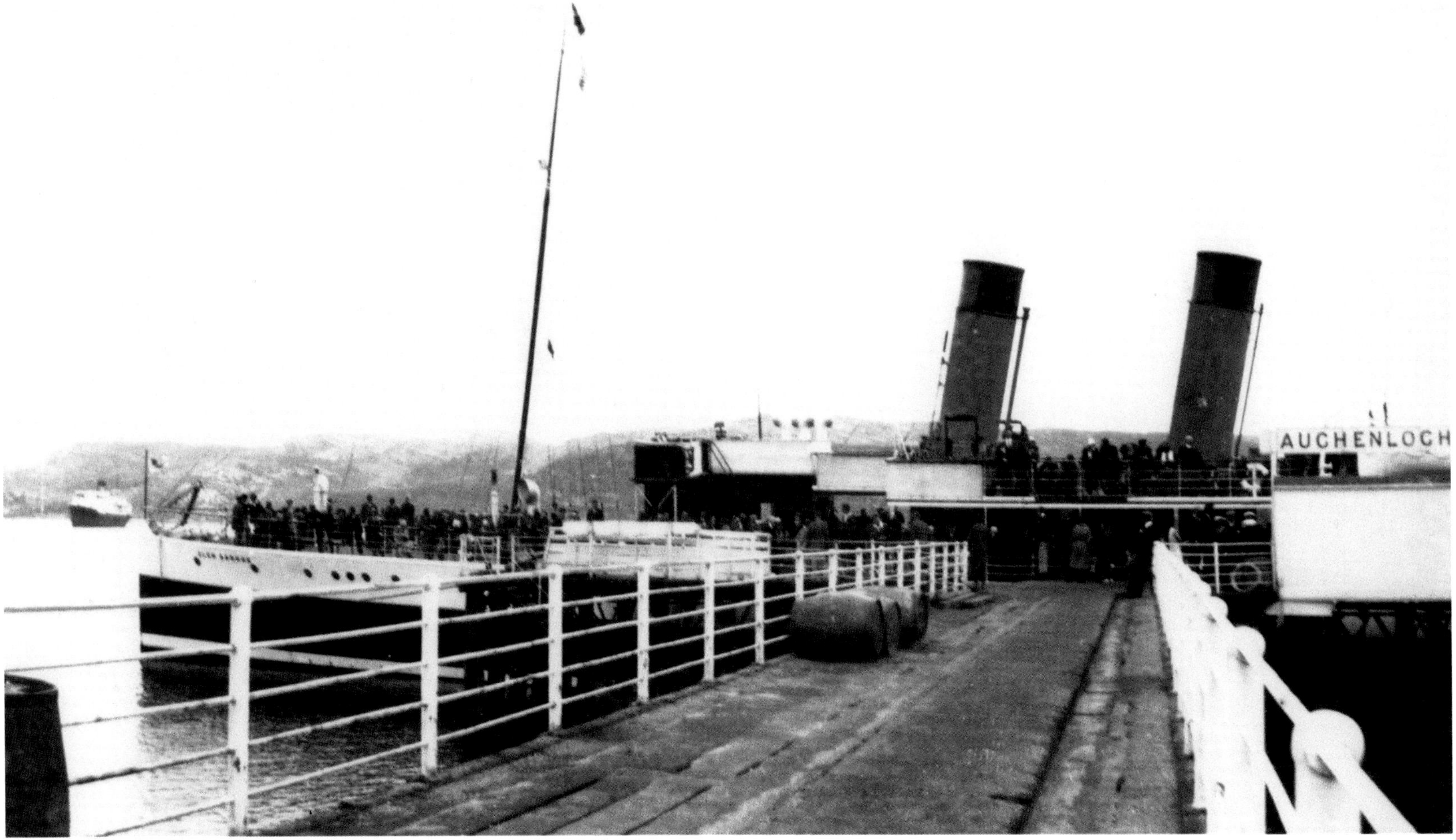

Turbine steamers usually had far more important work to do than visit Auchenlochan, and the London Midland and Scottish Railway's *Glen Sannox* was mostly to be found on the Ardrossan-Arran crossing for which she was built in 1925 – so this visit in July 1933 may have been for a special sailing or a service run for which she was unusually rostered. *Glen Sannox* was modelled on *Duchess of Argyll,* a steamer built nearly 20 years earlier, but did not represent a significant advance in style or appearance: she never achieved the popularity of the older vessel. Apart from a brief spell as a troop carrier on the Stranraer-Larne run during the Second World War, she remained on the Clyde until her withdrawal in 1953. The large ship anchored in the distance illustrates the West Kyle's historic role as a mooring ground for spare tonnage.

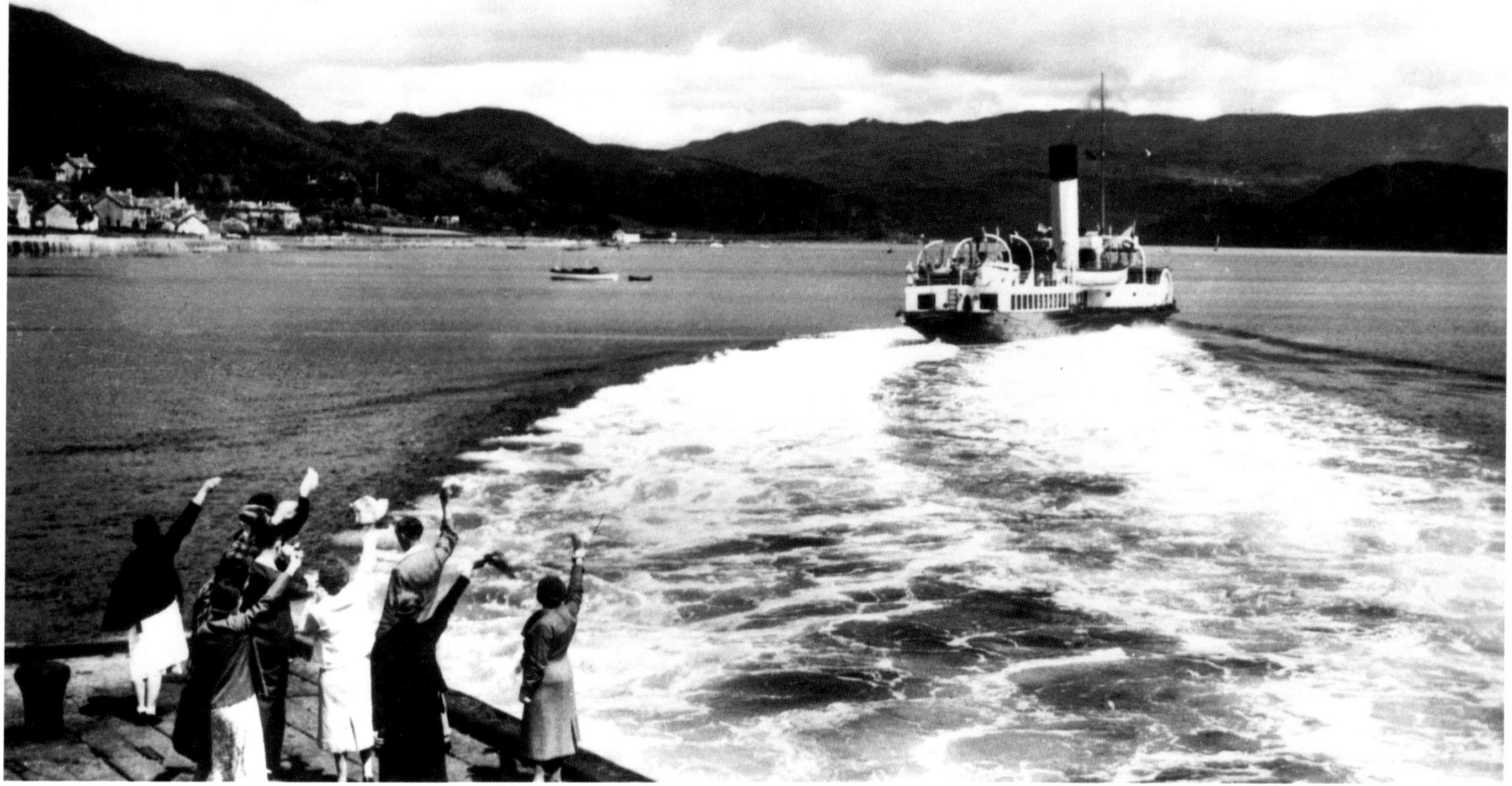

Farewell to the Kyles: there has always been something poignant about waving off a steamer from a small pier, as it whisks passengers away from unspoilt tranquillity towards the noise and bustle of the city. The 1930s scene here was replicated on an almost daily basis in summer from the 1880s to the 1960s. The pier is Tighnabruaich and the steamer is *Duchess of Rothesay*, departing on her afternoon return sailing to Gourock and Greenock. Built for the Caledonian Steam Packet Company in 1895, she almost became part of the Kyles scenery, initially operating the Arran via the Kyles cruise and latterly serving on the more bread-and-butter run from upper-firth railheads to Kyles piers. She served as a minesweeper in both world wars, but in 1945 was not considered worth reconditioning.

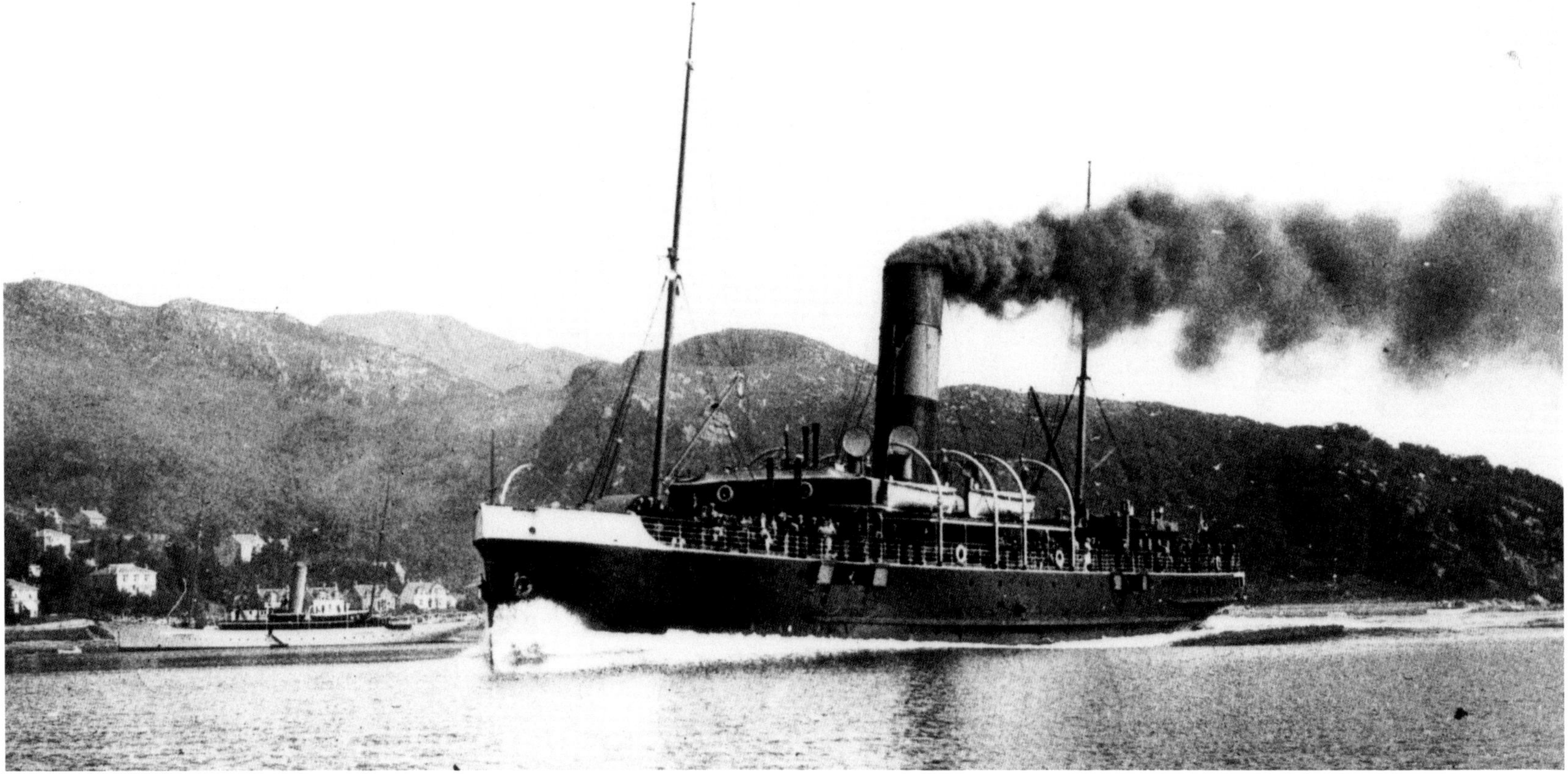

Dalriada steams past Tighnabruaich *circa* 1930, with one of the Clyde's elegant steam yachts at anchor on the left and the promontory at Rhubaan on the right. It was unusual to find a Campbeltown Company steamer in the Kyles of Bute: *Dalriada* and her older fleetmate *Davaar* usually made their daily voyage between Campbeltown and Glasgow via Garroch Head, heading in different directions on alternate days. On this occasion *Dalriada* was probably undertaking one of her there-and-back Saturday trips at the height of summer, sailing from Campbeltown as far as Gourock and Greenock in the morning, giving an excursion to Campbeltown via the Kyles in the afternoon, and returning up-firth to land her passengers at Gourock just before 10pm. Built at Port Glasgow in 1926, *Dalriada* lacked the yacht-like beauty of her Campbeltown Company predecessors, but with slanting stem, enormous funnel and two masts, she cut an imposing profile – and with a speed of 17 knots, she was reputedly the fastest single-screw steamer in the world. Her name, chosen by Campbeltown schoolchildren, recalled the ancient kingdom of which Kintyre was a part. The Campbeltown steamers were distinguishable by their funnel colouring of black-red-black. After ownership of *Dalriada* and *Davaar* passed to Clyde Cargo Steamers in 1937, they were given a plain red funnel with black top. Sent to the Thames as a salvage vessel in 1941, *Dalriada* was sunk there in June 1942.

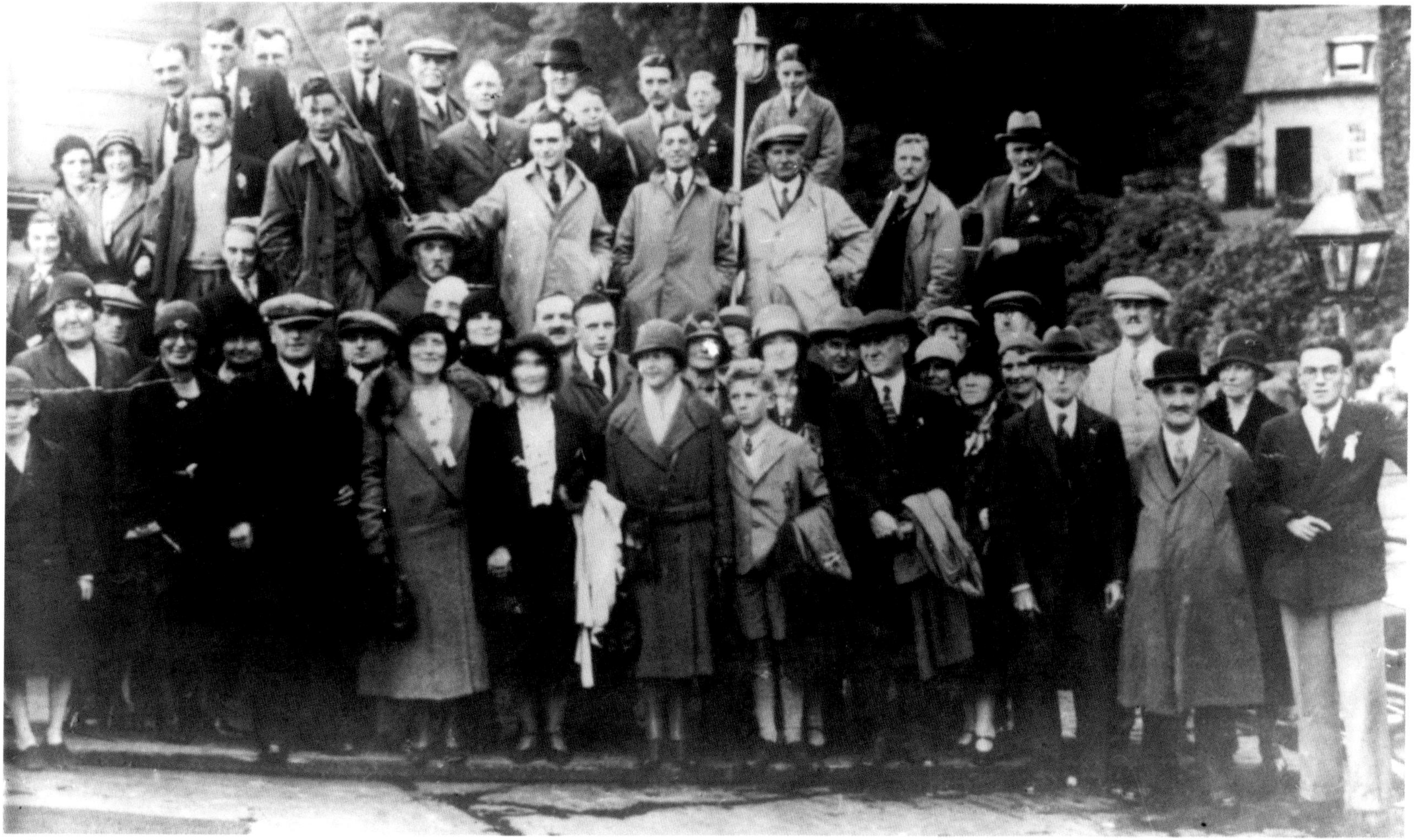

The setting was Ormidale, the date 6 August 1932 – two months after the formation in Glasgow of the Clyde River Steamer Club, the declared aim of which was to create opportunities for people interested in the Clyde steamer fleet to 'sail together, meet together, and talk together'. This trip to the Kyles of Bute was the club's first nominated excursion, and someone had the presence of mind to record it on camera. Members sailed on a timetabled service to Ormidale by the 1896 paddle steamer *Jupiter*, starting a tradition of organised outings that continues to this day. The club also hosts monthly meetings in winter at which speakers give illustrated talks on subjects of interest to shipping enthusiasts.

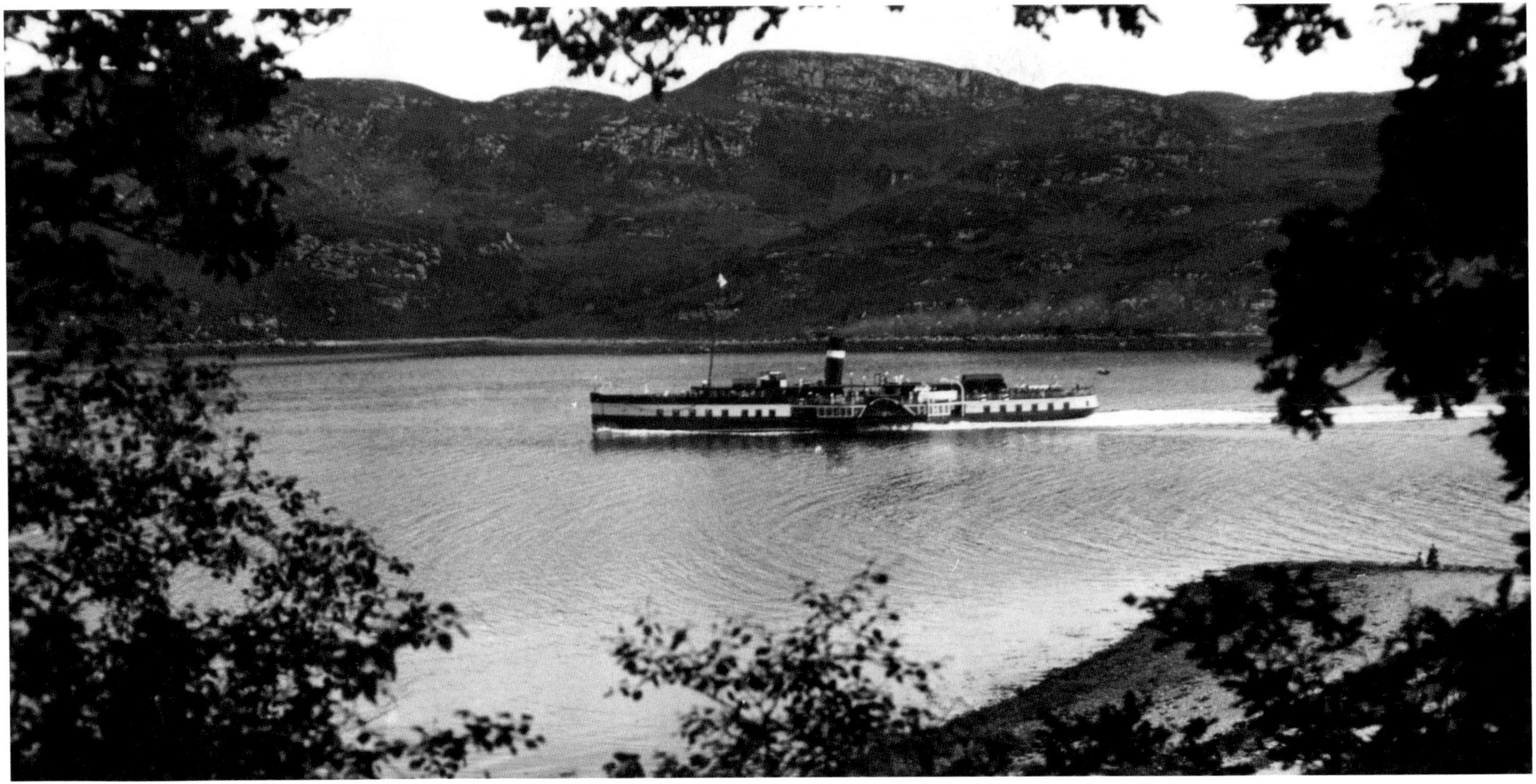

The most consistent photographer of Kyles scenes in the early and mid 20th century was Cuthbert Spencer (1873-1954), an Englishman by birth and long-time resident of Tighnabruaich, where he worked as a gardener. His picture postcards were eagerly snapped up by tourists, and many of them featured steamers. One of his favourite vantage points was the wooded cliff overlooking the promontory at Rhubaan, the trees of which provided a natural frame for the succession of passing steamers. Spencer's photograph of *Talisman* dates from 1935, her first season. A year later, in common with the rest of the London and North Eastern Railway's Clyde fleet, she appeared in a light grey hull, and after the war, once again with black hull, she received a covered wheelhouse. *Talisman* was the Clyde's first and only diesel-electric paddle vessel. In place of the traditional open engine room, with powerful cranks for everyone to admire, her English Electric Company machinery was hidden behind a windowed house on the main deck, its motor controlled directly by the ship's Master on the bridge – cleaner and more fuel-efficient than steam-driven paddlers but also less exciting to the eye. *Talisman* served her owners well on the Craigendoran-Kyles run up to midsummer 1939, when she broke down. She gave distinguished war service and, after re-engining in 1953, became the Millport boat, cruising to Tighnabruaich every Sunday in summer until her withdrawal at the end of the 1966 season.

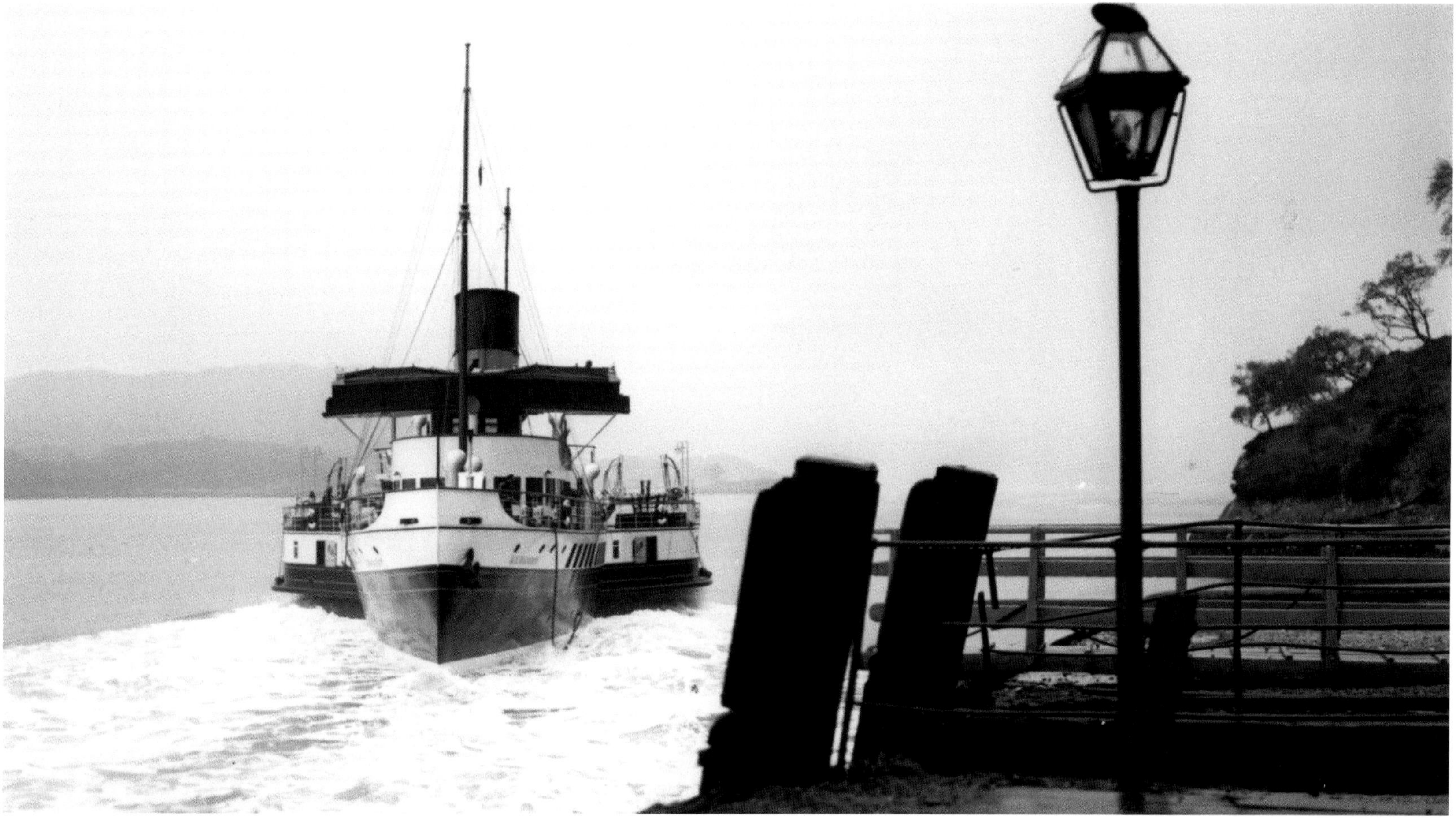

Mercury leaves Ormidale in the late 1930s. This atmospheric photograph captures the isolation of the Loch Riddon pier at a time when it was becoming increasingly hard to justify its inclusion in the Kyles timetable: there was simply not enough traffic, and the pier dropped off the schedule on the outbreak of war in September 1939. *Mercury* and her sister ship *Caledonia*, built in 1934 as replacements for older, similarly named steamers, were big passenger carriers that proved as useful on upper-firth ferry crossings as on down-firth excursions. They introduced a controversial design feature – concealed paddle boxes – which became the 'trademark' of the London Midland and Scottish Railway's Clyde paddlers in the 1930s. *Mercury*'s life was short: requisitioned soon after war was declared, she was minesweeping off southern Ireland on Christmas Day 1940 when a mine became caught in her sweeping equipment and exploded, causing extensive damage. Despite attempts to tow her to Milford Haven, she sank within five hours. There were no casualties.

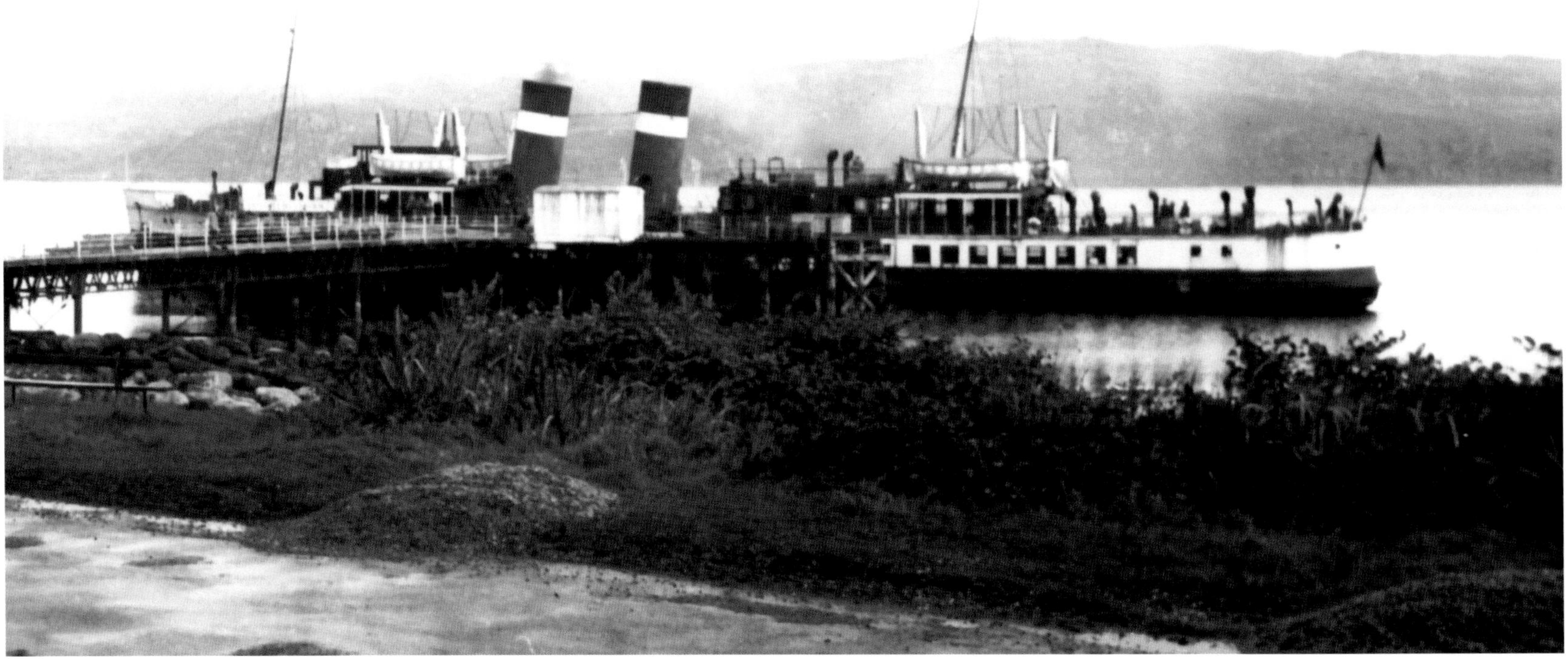

Waverley makes an unusual sight at Auchenlochan in 1947, her first season. That summer she was to be found far more often on the Craigendoran-Arrochar excursion, for which she was built, than on the daily Kyles service, which the London and North Eastern Railway had revived in 1946 on a seasonal basis. After the UK's railway companies were nationalised on 1 January 1948, ownership of the Craigendoran fleet passed to the British Transport Commission. *Waverley*'s funnels were painted yellow with black top. It was only after the Paddle Steamer Preservation Society bought *Waverley* for £1 in 1974 that her original funnel colours were restored. Auchenlochan Pier closed after the 1948 season, but it was not until 2001 that its remains were demolished.

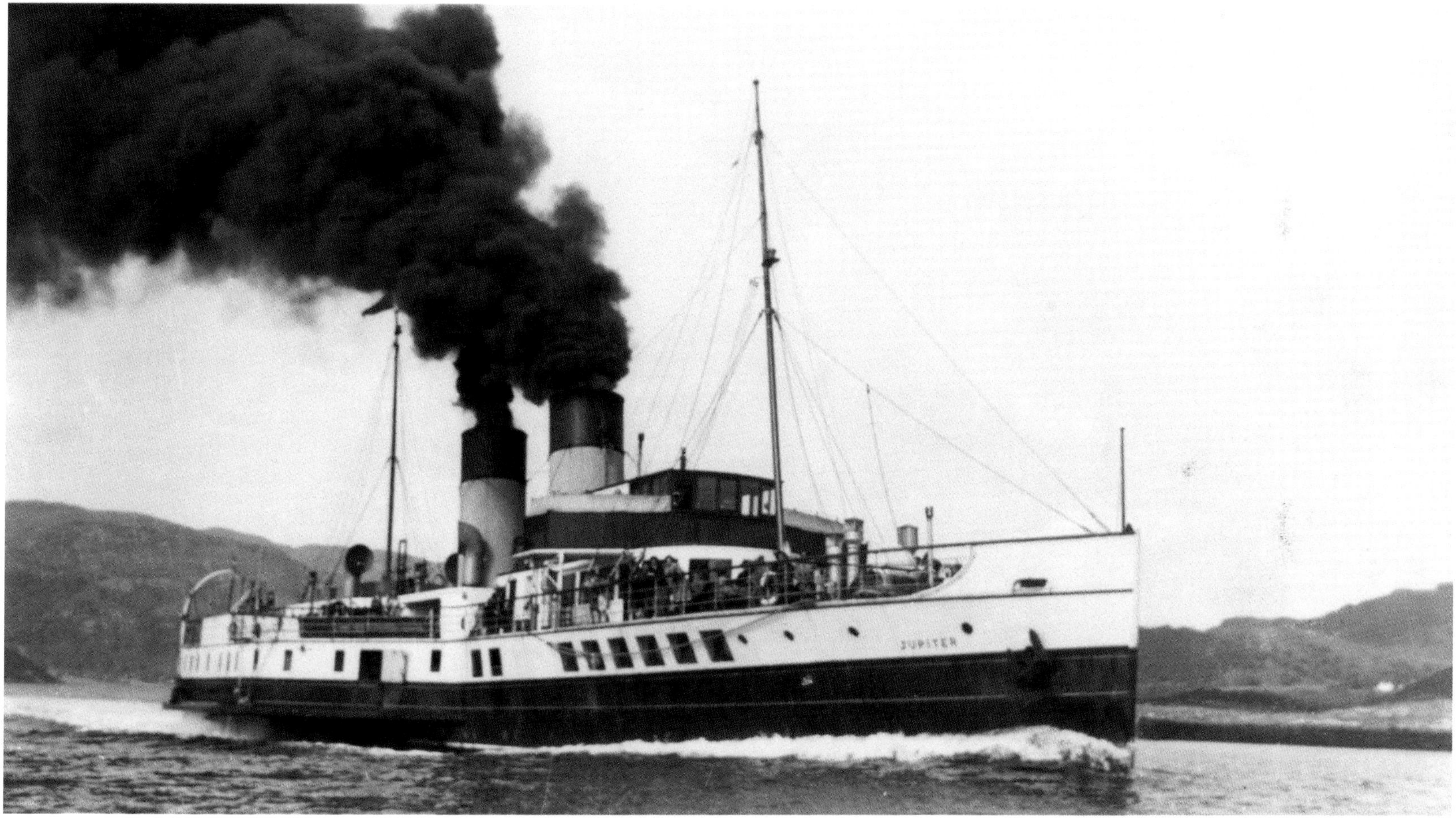

Jupiter steams through the dogleg channel of the Narrows in 1949 on her way back to Rothesay from Tighnabruaich. The photograph, probably taken from a small boat or yacht, conveys an impression of power and speed – the opposite of *Jupiter*'s post-war reputation. Built at Govan in 1937 she was a finely proportioned vessel, with the enclosed paddle-boxes favoured by the LMS in the 1930s, but she was never a flyer. Her roomy accommodation was designed for moving large crowds on the bread-and-butter ferry routes of the upper Firth, and only occasionally did she venture further afield. With black smoke pouring from her funnels, this is clearly a coal-fired steamer. Despite being converted to oil-firing in 1956-57, *Jupiter* was withdrawn the following winter as part of the Caledonian Steam Packet Company's fleet rationalisation programme. She languished in Greenock's Albert Harbour until 1961, when she was towed to Dublin for scrapping.

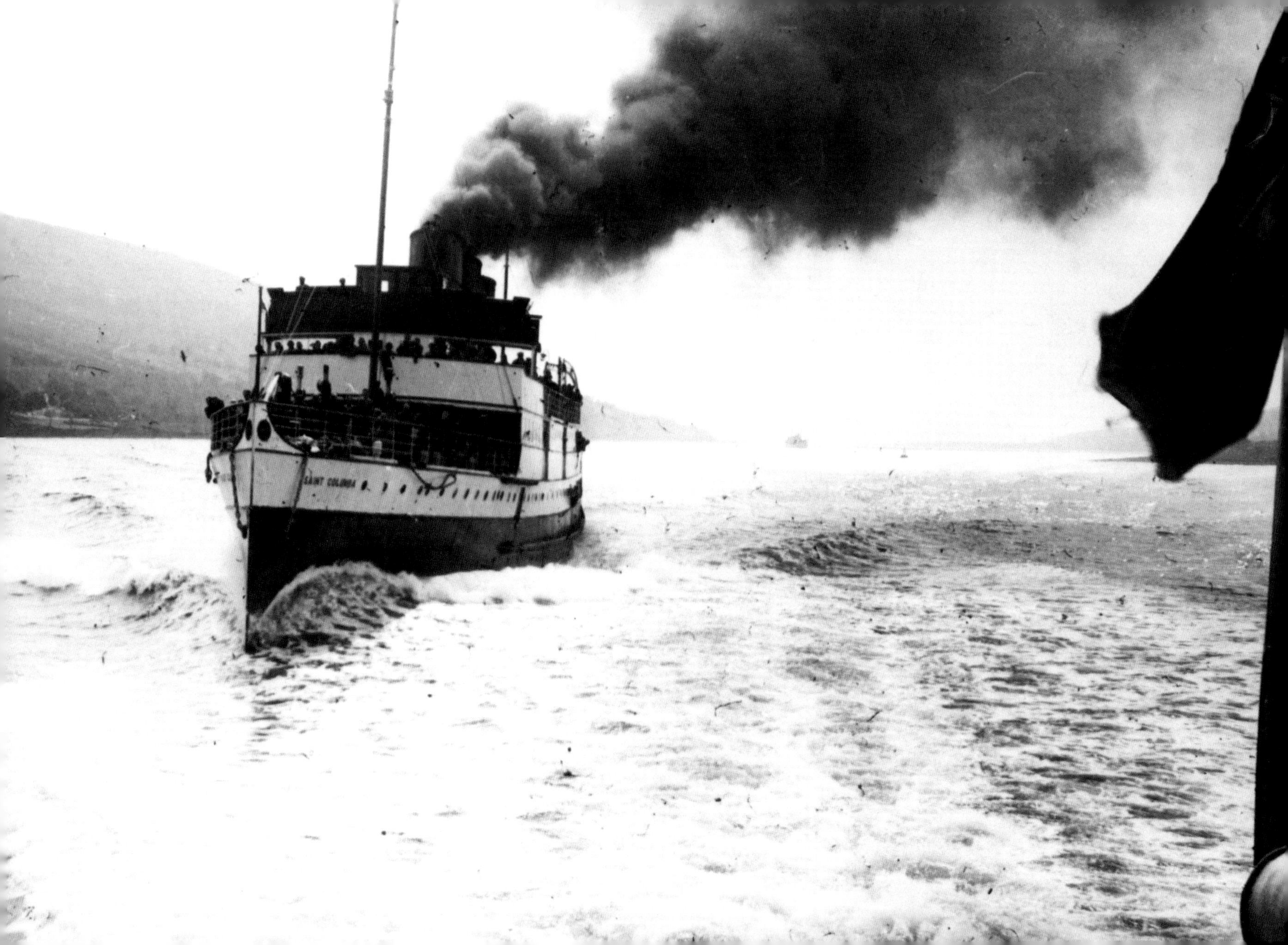

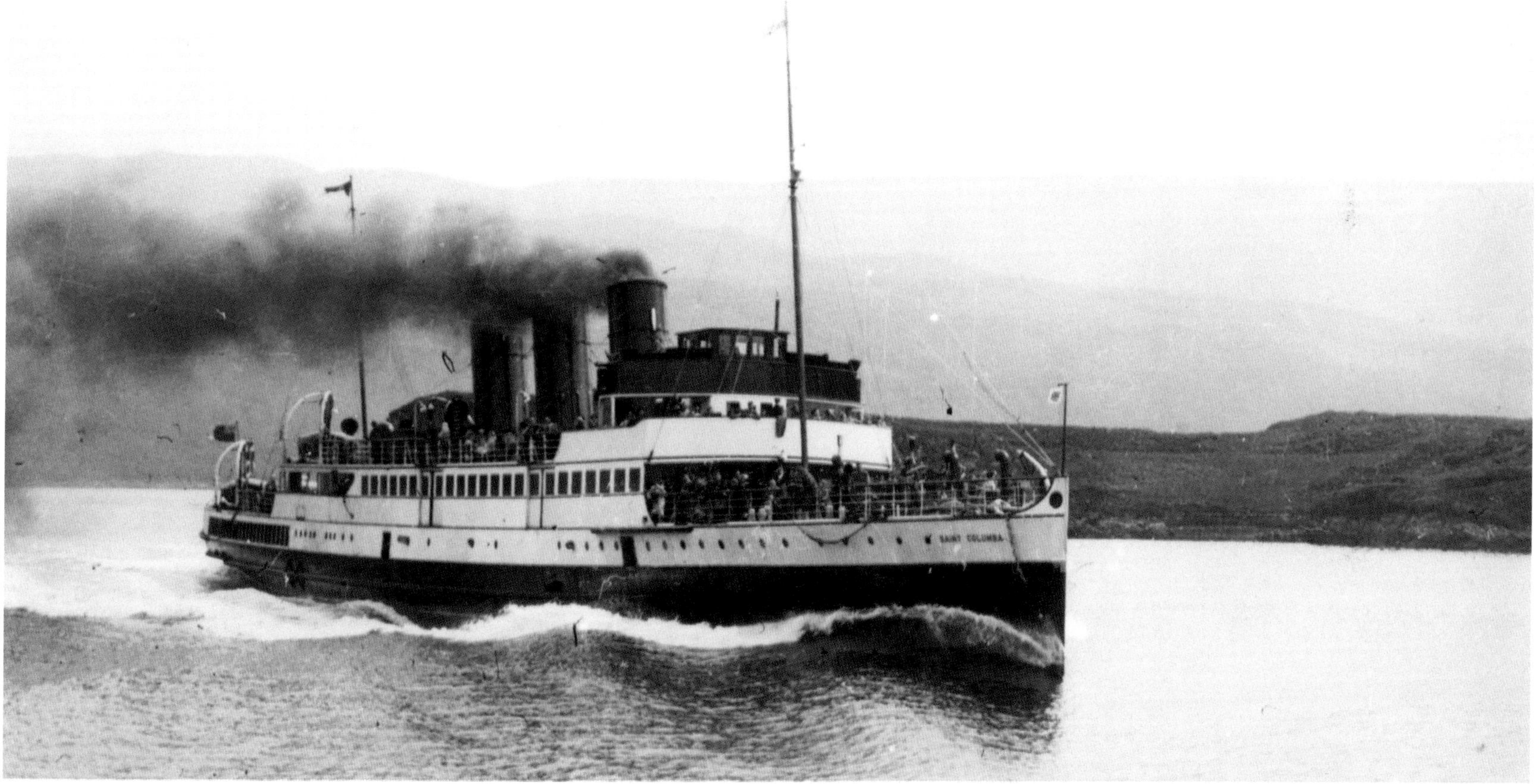

The 1950s saw some famous races in the Kyles of Bute between two of the Clyde's fastest steamers, the Caledonian Steam Packet Company's *Duchess of Montrose* en route to Arran and MacBrayne's *Saint Columba* on the Ardrishaig mail run. Both were turbines, but whereas *Saint Columba* had been converted to oil-firing before the war, the 'Montrose' was still coal-fired and often suffered from poor quality of coal. Their ding-dong battle on Wednesday 12 July 1950 was documented by Geoffrey Grimshaw, who photographed the three-funnelled MacBrayne ship trying to overtake the 'Montrose' in the East Kyle (facing page) and after passing through the Narrows (this page). He later recalled how *Duchess of Montrose* "cleared Rothesay at 10.45, ten minutes late. *Saint Columba,* running 20 minutes late, cleared at 10.50 and there seemed every possibility that she would beat the 'Montrose' into Tighnabruaich. From Rothesay onwards the 'Montrose' really pushed. Blessed with good coal she managed to keep her lead to the Narrows after which *Saint Columba* had no time to get ahead. Hard steaming with the coal burners usually meant smoke. This day was no exception. As the 'Montrose' drove up the Kyles of Bute, her smoke poured astern in a thick black cloud, almost obliterating the following *Saint Columba.*"

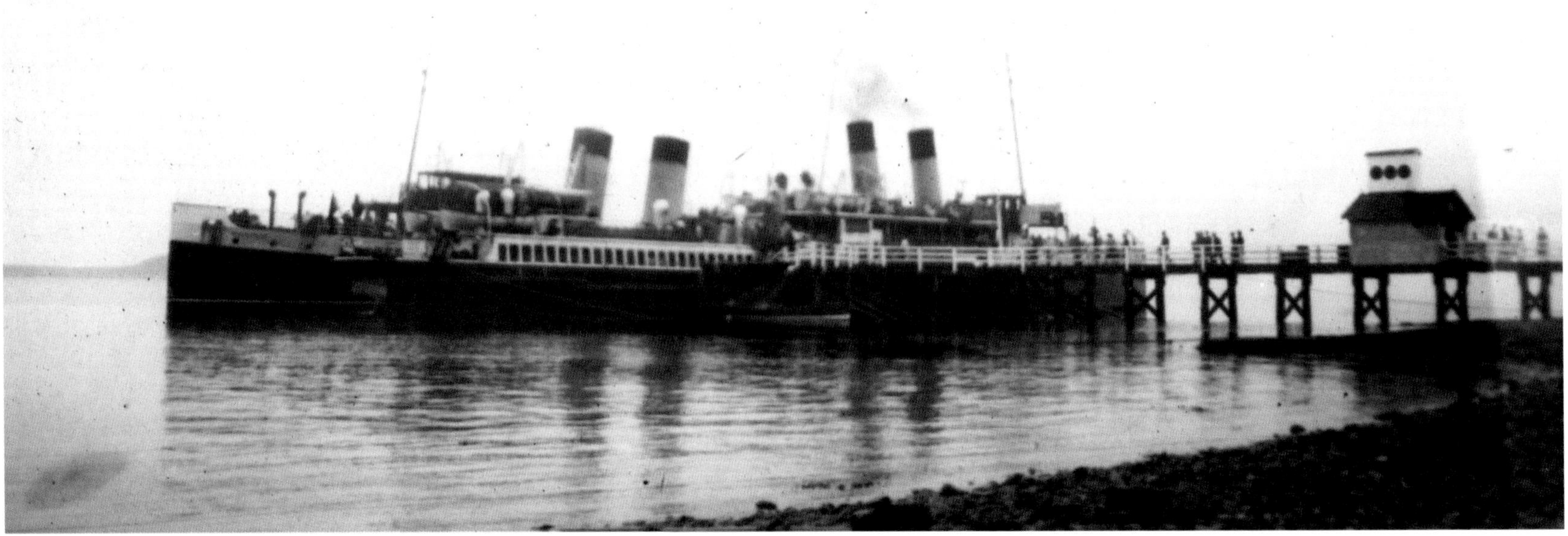

Exactly why *Jeanie Deans* berthed alongside *King Edward* at Tighnabruaich is not known, but the 'Edward' was probably on the daily 'doon the watter' sailing to the Kyles from Glasgow and 'Jeanie' on her way back from the weekday Round Bute cruise. Whatever the case, it was rare to find two excursion steamers berthed together at any Kyles pier. 'Jeanie' is in post-1947 nationalised colours and has canvas bridge dodgers, which suggests the photo was taken in the summer of 1948 or 1949. Two years later *King Edward* was withdrawn. Built by Denny of Dumbarton in 1901 she was the world's first passenger-carrying turbine steamer – so revolutionary that her builders had plans to convert her into a paddle steamer if the experiment did not work satisfactorily. She pioneered the daytime return sailing from upper-firth piers to Campbeltown, travelled to Russia's White Sea in the First World War and served as a troop tender on the Clyde in the Second World War.

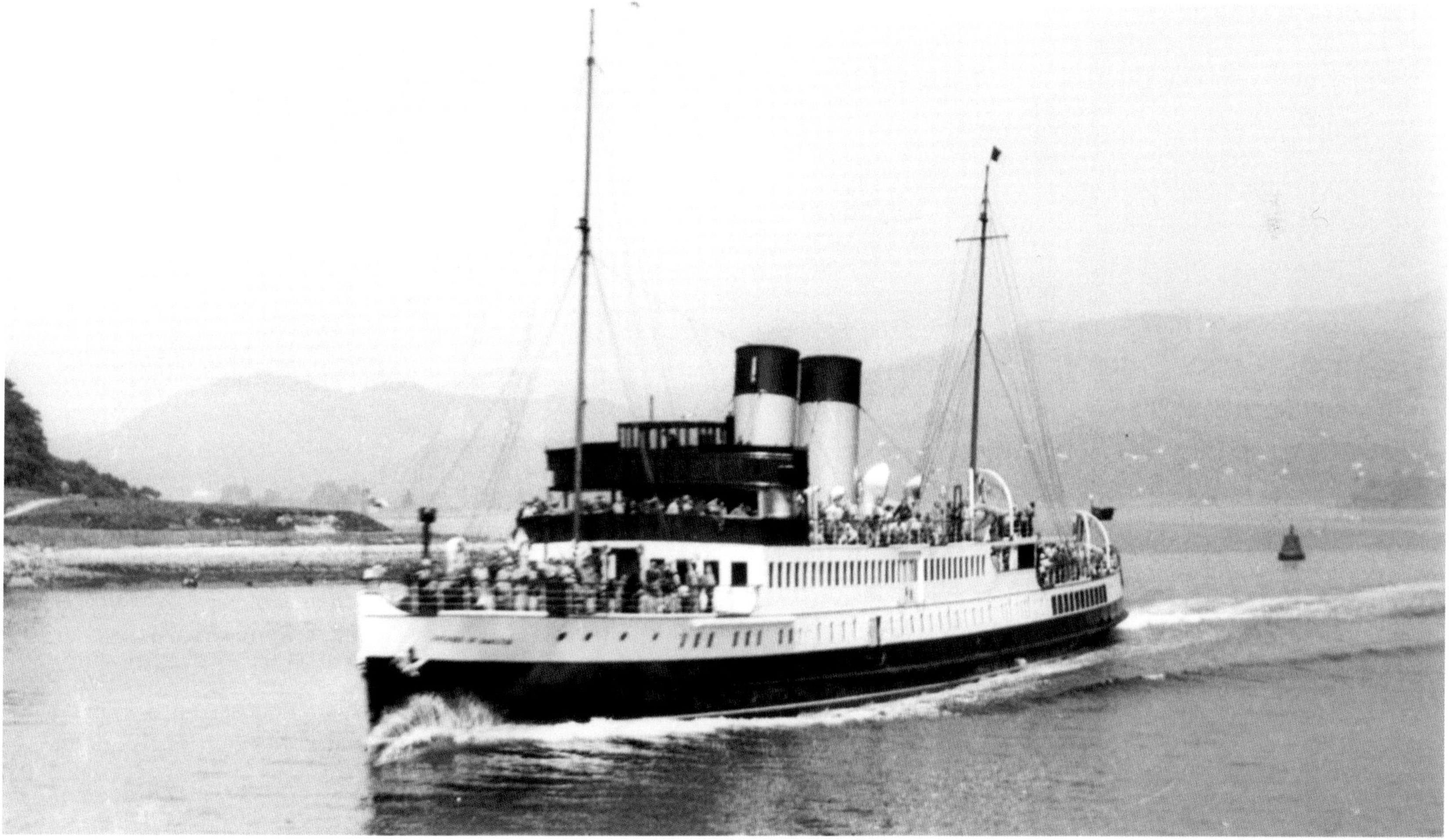

Duchess of Hamilton glides past Rhubaan on her way in to Tighnabruaich Pier on a glorious summer morning in the mid 1950s. The younger sister of *Duchess of Montrose*, the 'Hamilton' was built in 1932 to give cruises out of Ayr. After 1945 she became a partner of the 'Montrose' on the long-distance cruise roster from Gourock. In this role she quickly emerged as the Caledonian Steam Packet Company's unofficial flagship – largely thanks to Captain Fergus Murdoch, her fiercely competitive and punctilious Master from 1946 until 1967. Best known on the Campbeltown run, *Duchess of Hamilton* also undertook the Wednesday Arran via the Kyles sailing. For anyone boarding the ship at Tighnabruaich, a special return connection was provided from Rothesay in the evening by a smaller steamer, advertised as an evening cruise to the Kyles for holidaymakers on Bute.

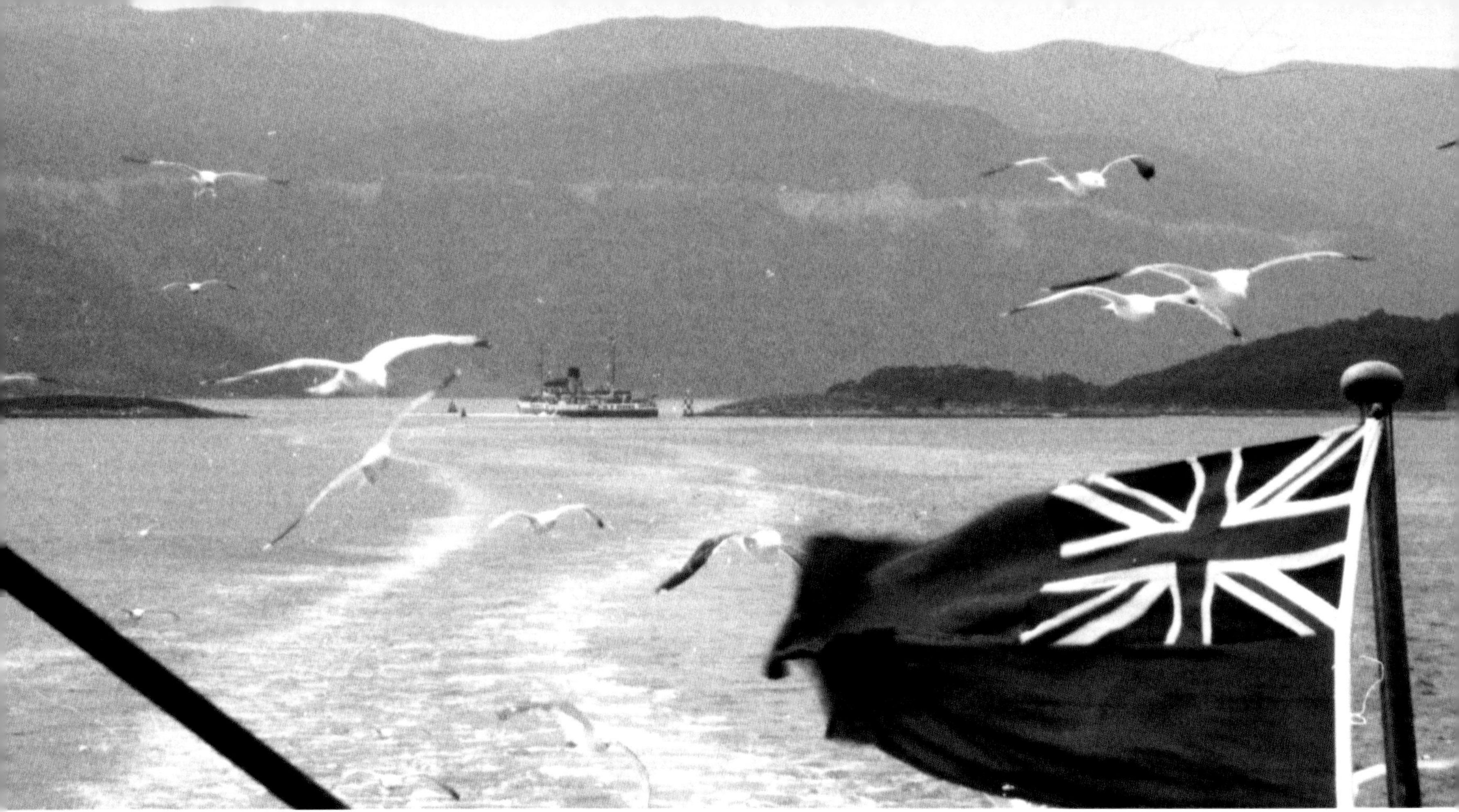

With little room for manoeuvre on either side, Clyde steamer captains have always treated the Narrows with respect, slowing down and maintaining a straight course until clear of the rocks. It is unusual, therefore, to find *Caledonia* astride the Burnt Islands and going astern – a bizarre, not to say risky manoeuvre. There is no steamer approaching in the opposite direction to stop her in her tracks. It is well documented that on Sunday 7 July 1957, while on a cruise from Ayr and Troon to Rothesay and the Kyles, *Caledonia* broke down: passengers thought she had blundered onto the rocks. It seems that for a few minutes she was grounded before managing to pull herself free. Although she returned to Ayr unassisted, she was out of service for the following five weeks. The occasion recorded here, however, shows the hillside scar created by 'the new road' in 1969, indicating this photo dates from an unexplained incident shortly before *Caledonia* was finally withdrawn from service in October that year.

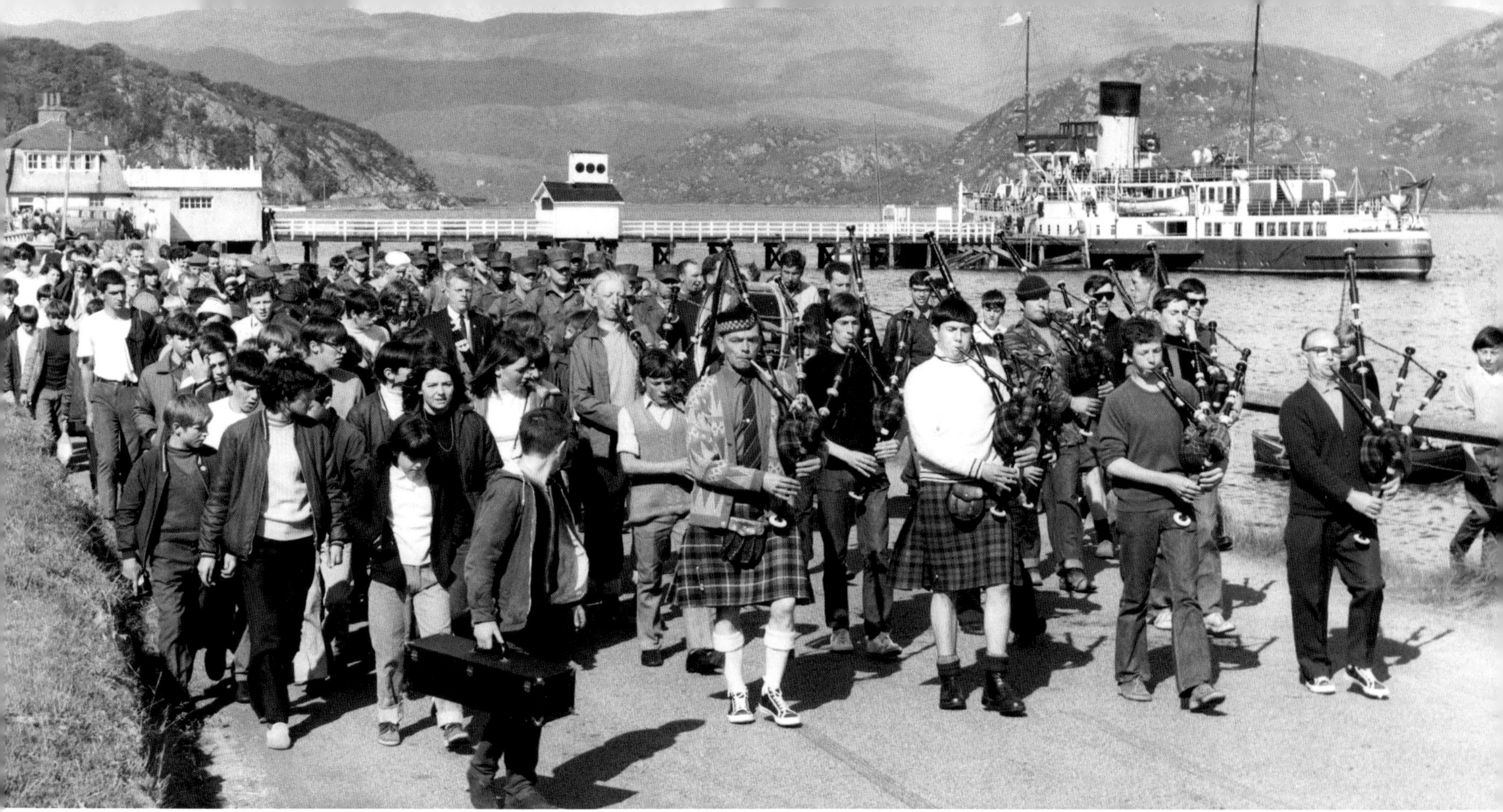

In their heyday Clyde piers were not just an essential link between coastal communities and the wider world. They also had a social function – as a hub of communal activity. The scene here illustrates that role. The year is 1969, *Caledonia*'s last in service, and Saturday 21 June is the day of the Tighnabruaich to Dunoon walk. According to a local newspaper report the following week, the event "attracted a large entry. Travelling by steamer from Dunoon the party were headed by Dunoon Argyll Pipe Band, who played them from Tighnabruaich pier end to the Police Brae [better known today as Bobby's Brae], where the walk commenced at 5.25 after Miss Euphemia Lamont, Millhouse, had cut the tartan ribbon at the starting point. It ended in a road race instead of a pedestrian hike, winner Tim Winters, Benmore Adventure Centre, covering the distance in less than four hours." The Tighnabruaich to Dunoon walk is no more. Its modern equivalent is the 'Kyles 10 miles' road race, starting where Auchenlochan Pier used to be, heading south round Ardlamont and finishing at Kames Hotel.

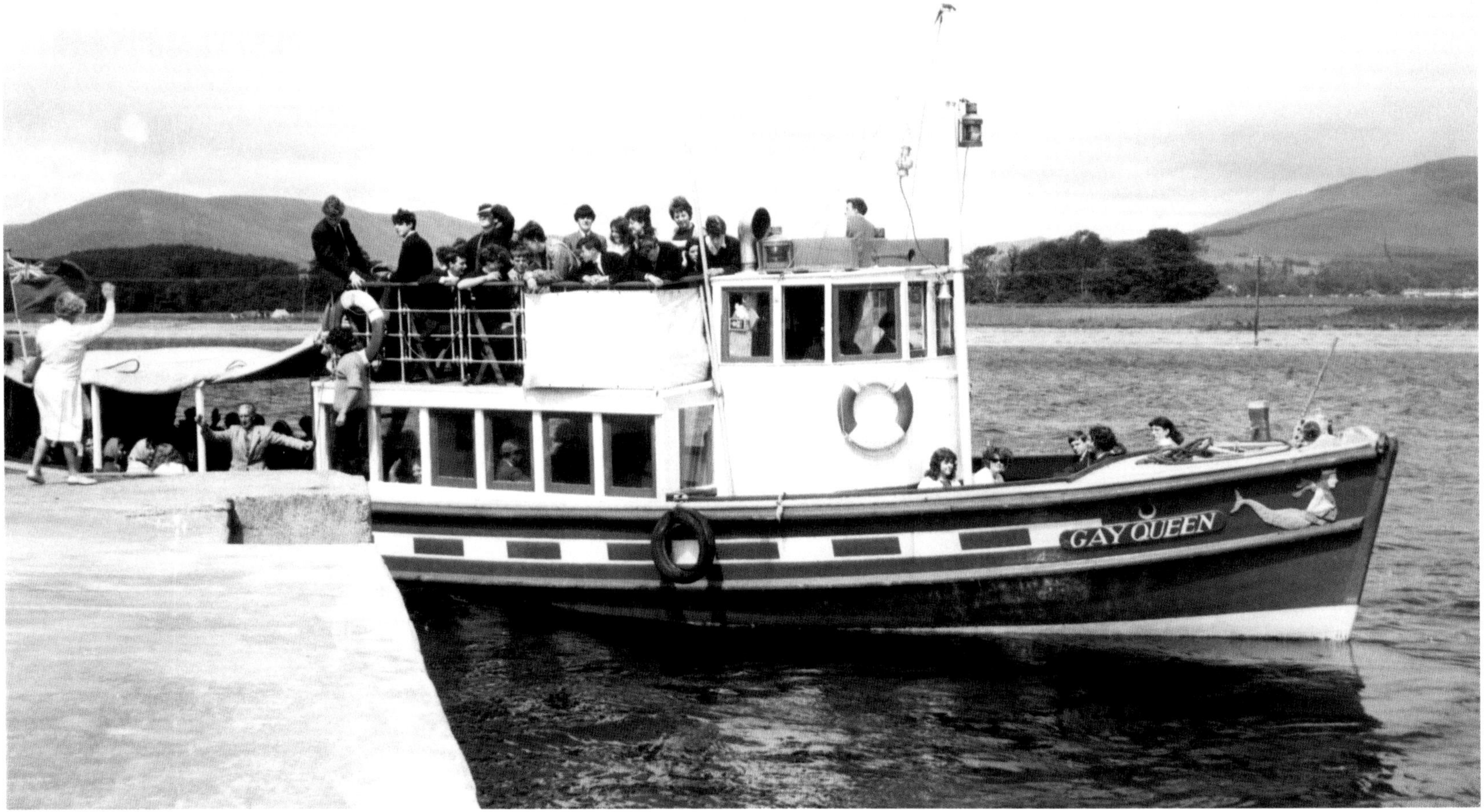

If you were on holiday at Rothesay in the 1950s and 60s, the week or fortnight could not go by without a trip to the Kyles of Bute aboard *Gay Queen*, a wooden-hulled vessel with red colour scheme and no funnel. These trips were short, usually non-landing and invariably enlivened by the singing of her skipper, Herbert McIver. *Gay Queen* left from a jetty opposite the Rothesay Pavilion, and while the Kyles were the most popular destination, she sometimes visited other places in the neighbourhood – as on this occasion, which finds her at the stone jetty at Toward on the Cowal Peninsula opposite Rothesay Bay. She was sold to Poole in 1988.

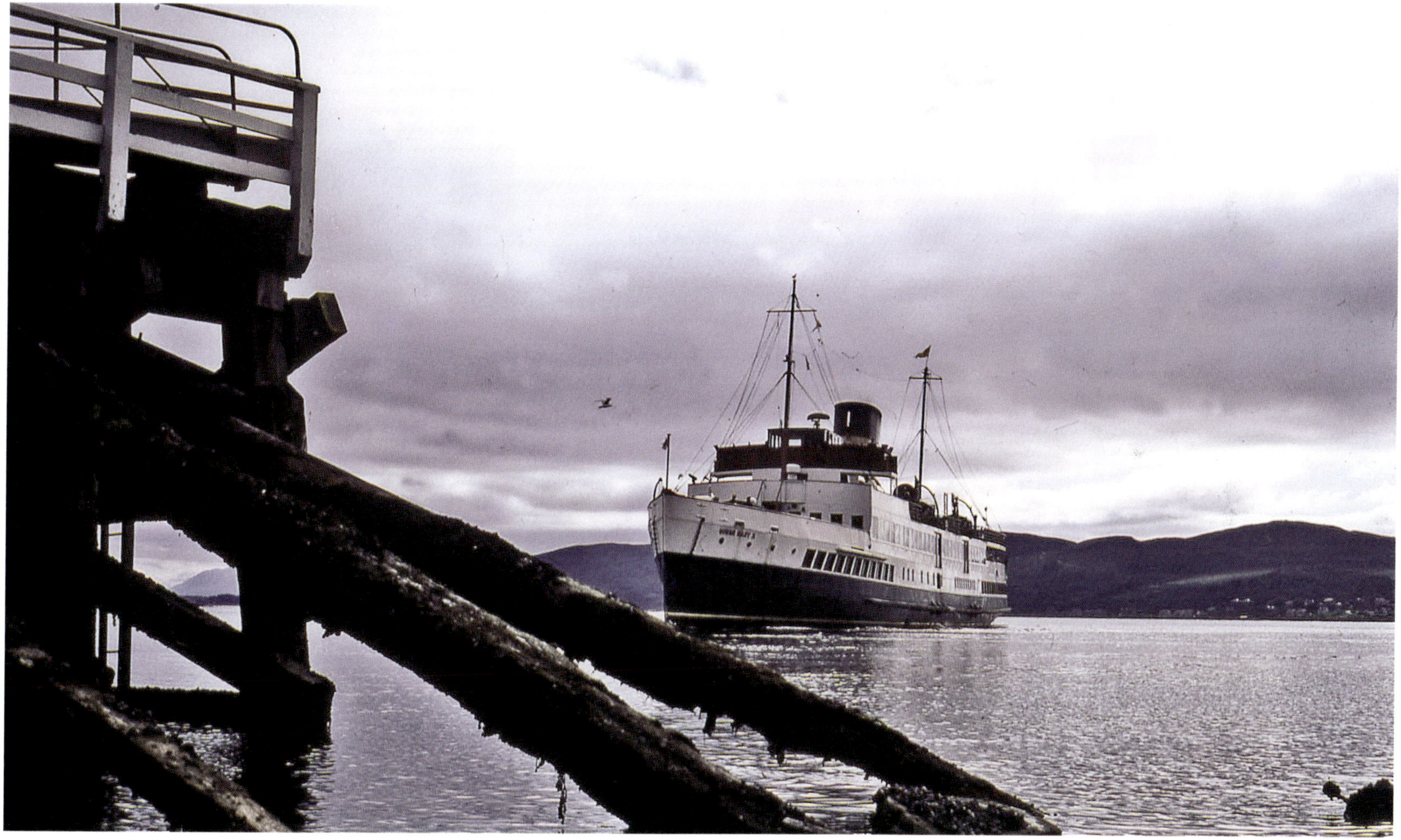

For generations of Glaswegians, the leisurely journey by steamer down the River Clyde to the Kyles of Bute represented not only a change of landscape but a release from everyday life. In the 1950s and 60s, when day-trippers arrived at Tighnabruaich Pier aboard *Queen Mary II,* they were stepping into a different universe – the rarefied air of the Highlands, a world of tranquillity, far from the hustle and bustle of home (albeit sometimes plagued by midges). A gentle walk along the front had a restorative effect. While trippers enjoyed their hour ashore, the steamer cast off to let MacBrayne's Ardrishaig mail boat call, and then came back facing in the direction of homeward travel – a ritual illustrated by this photograph from the late 1960s.

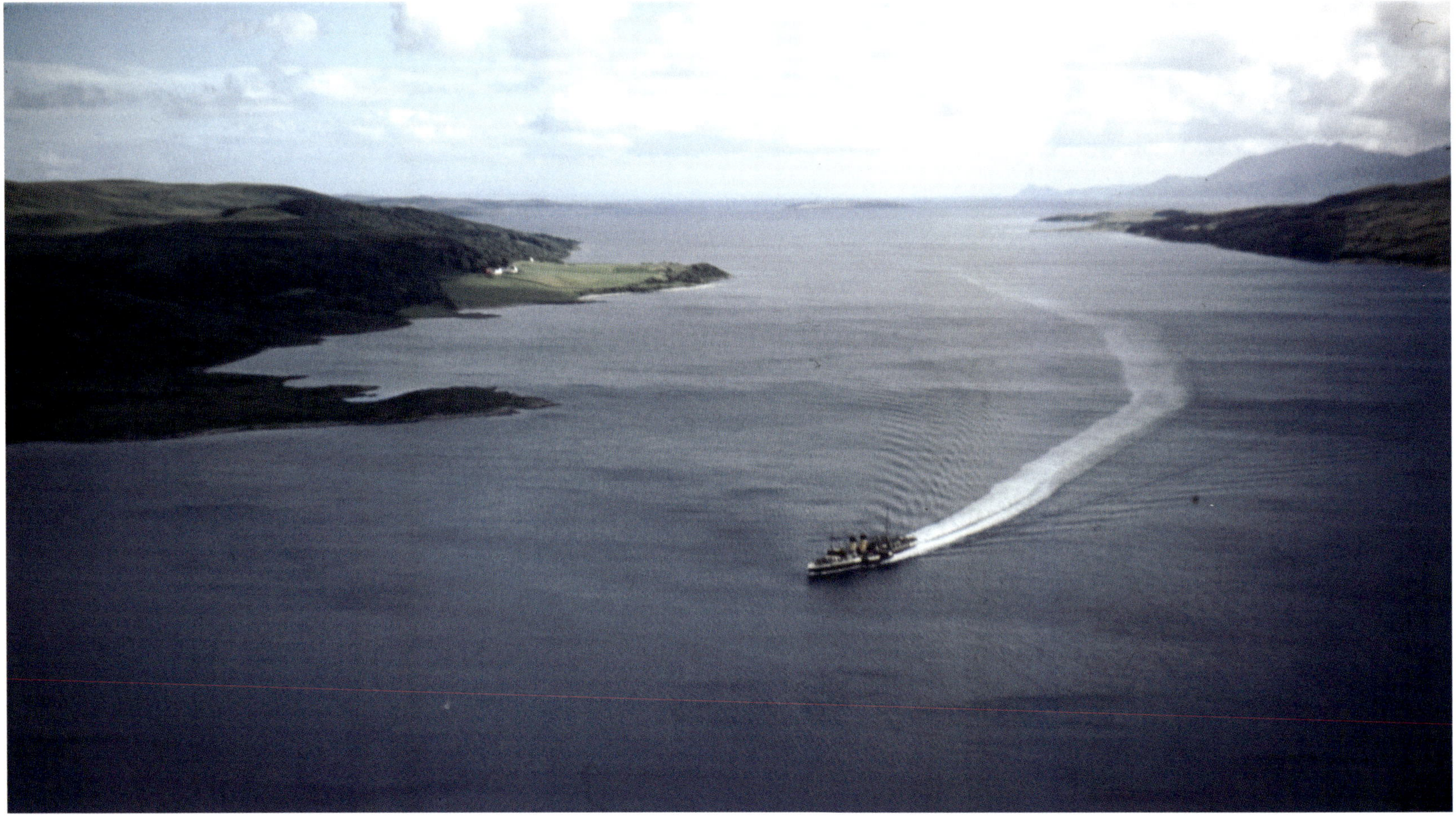

In the post-war era one of the most regular visitors to the Kyles was *Jeanie Deans*, pictured advancing up the West Kyle towards Tighnabruaich Pier on her Round Bute cruise. Every weekday she would leave Craigendoran at 12.40, usually with busloads of trippers aboard, and call at Gourock, Dunoon, Innellan and Rothesay, before rounding Garroch Head and heading north through Inchmarnock Sound to the Kyles and back to Rothesay. It was a pedestrian existence for a steamer that had visited all corners of the Firth in her 1930s heyday, but 'Jeanie' was no longer the flyer of her youth. She nevertheless had a grandeur and stateliness missing from *Waverley*, her post-war Craigendoran fleetmate. Withdrawn at the end of the 1964 season, 'Jeanie' was sold the following year to a London businessman. Attempts to operate her as a Thames excursion steamer in the summers of 1966 and 1967 failed miserably, and she was broken up in Belgium.

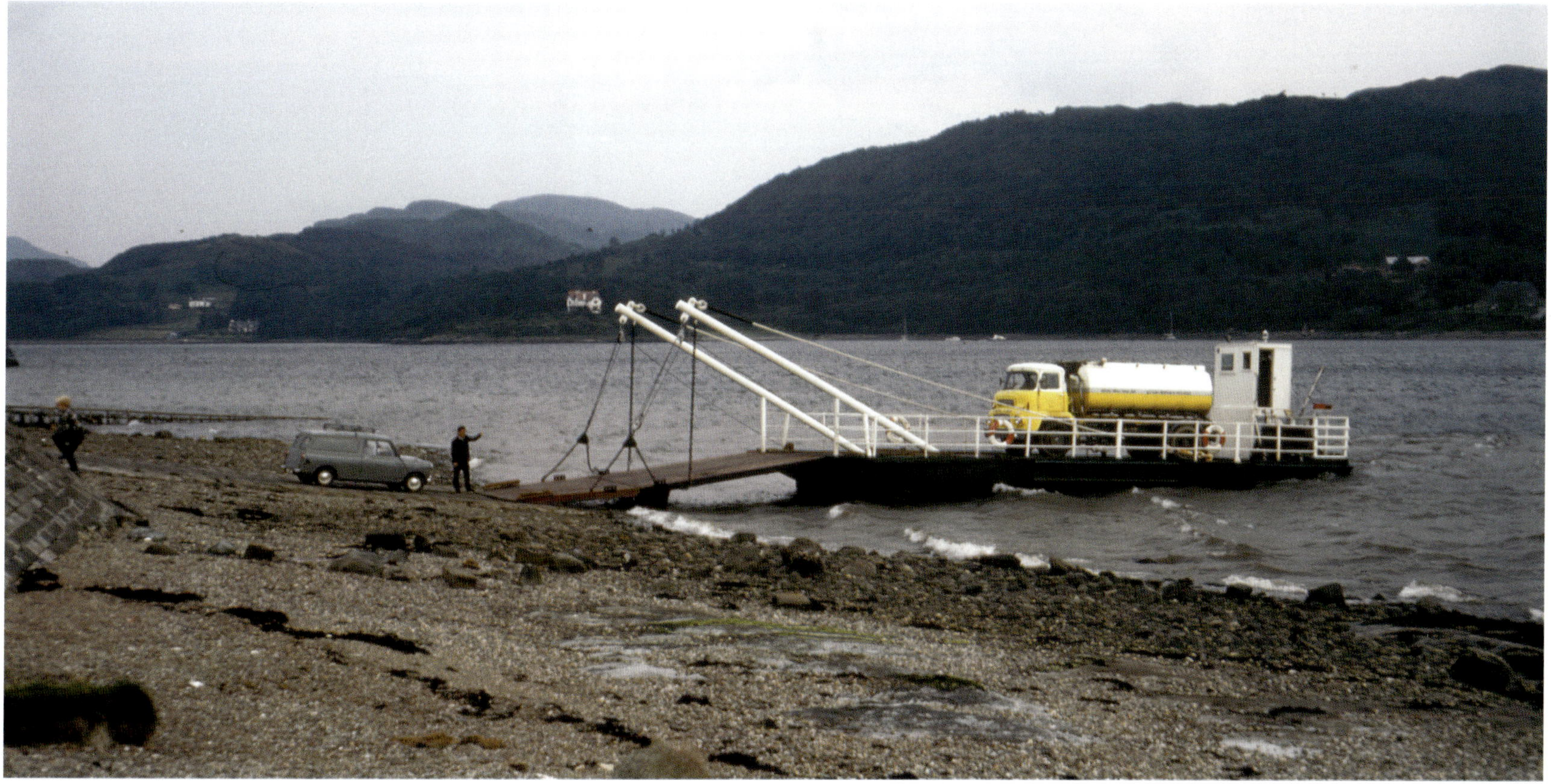

The earliest known reference to a ferry across the East Kyle is in 1685, when James Boill, 'ferryor in Ardintraive', had his ferryboats, nets and furniture confiscated in reprisal for the Earl of Argyll's Rising. The ferry is mentioned again in 1783 in connection with building a road 'in Rue to the ferrying place'. The Colintraive ferry became more important during the early 19th century Loch Fyne herring boom: between 1805 and 1811 a road was built from Loch Fyne through Glendaruel to Colintraive, enabling faster communication between Inveraray and Glasgow via Colintraive and Rothesay. It was not until July 1950 that a car ferry service across the East Kyle began – a primitive affair, with a former wartime landing craft (capacity: four cars) and wire matting on the beach. This photograph at Rhubodach dates from the late 1960s, when things were still pretty rudimentary. It shows *Dhuirinish*, a former Loch Etive ferry that came to Colintraive in 1967 and sank during a gale on the night of 14 January 1968. She was raised and refitted, before resuming service that summer. In December 1969 the Bute Ferry Company sold out to the Caledonian Steam Packet Company, which put the 10-car *Portree*, a former Skye ferry, on the run in June 1970, with *Dhuirinish* remaining until the following year. CalMac's new 'Loch' class of drive-through ferries, with capacity for 12 cars, took over the service in 1986.

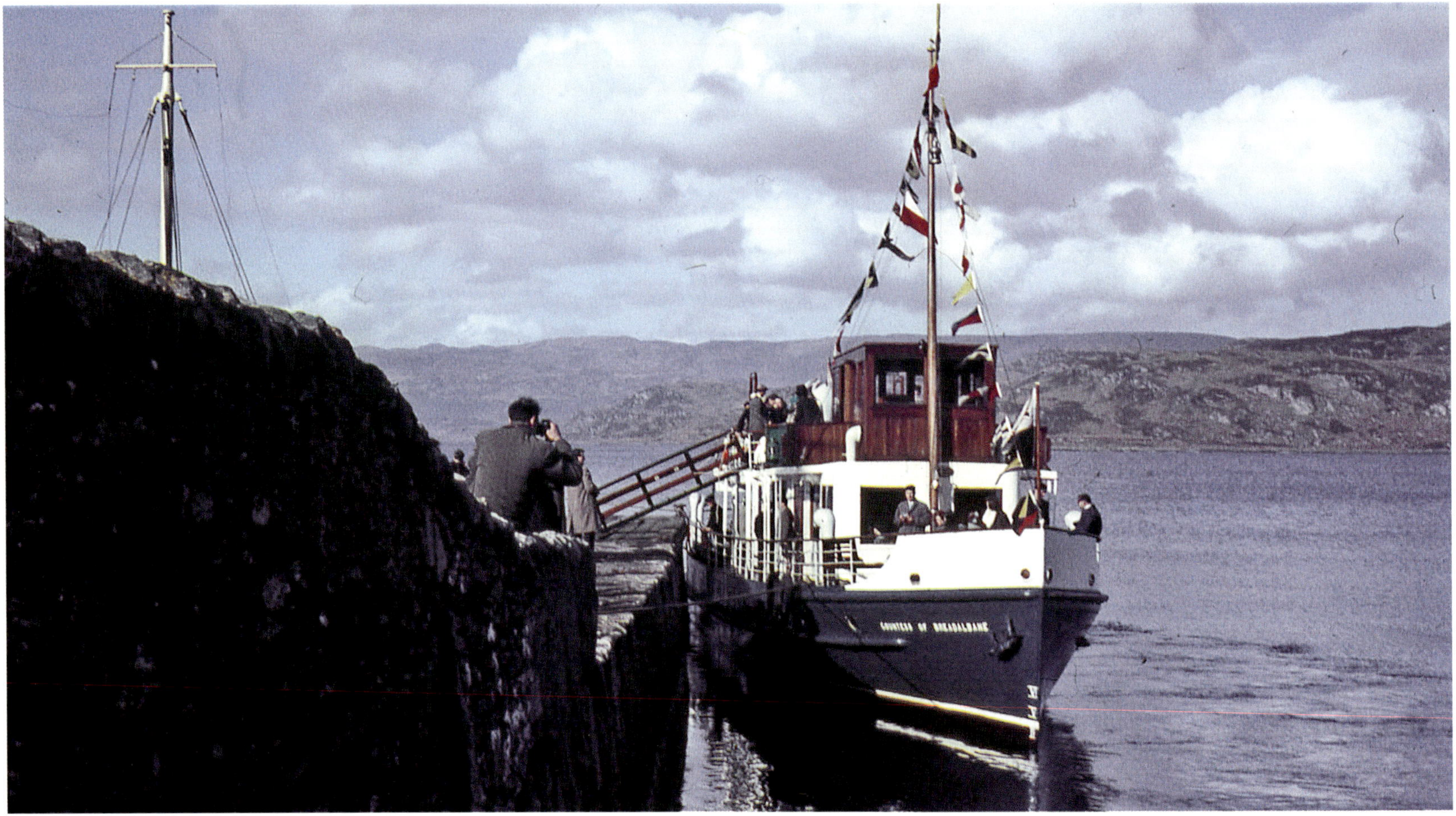

On 14 May 1966 *Countess of Breadalbane* became the first Clyde 'steamer' since the 1920s to visit Kames. She berthed at the stone cargo quay, a few yards north of where the old steamer pier was situated. The occasion was a Clyde River Steamer Club charter from Craigendoran and Gourock to the Kyles – one of several such charters in the 1960s taking in places that had dropped off the steamer map over the previous quarter-century. The 'Breadalbane' had a most unusual history. Built by Denny of Dumbarton in 1936 for the LMS's tourist sailings on Loch Awe, she was transported by road to the Clyde in 1952 and undertook a variety of duties for the CSP until 1971, when she was sold to Gourock ferrymaster Roy Ritchie and subsequently to owners operating out of Oban. In 1982 she made her second overland journey – this time to Loch Lomond, giving excursions there until the late 1990s. In 1999 she was scrapped.

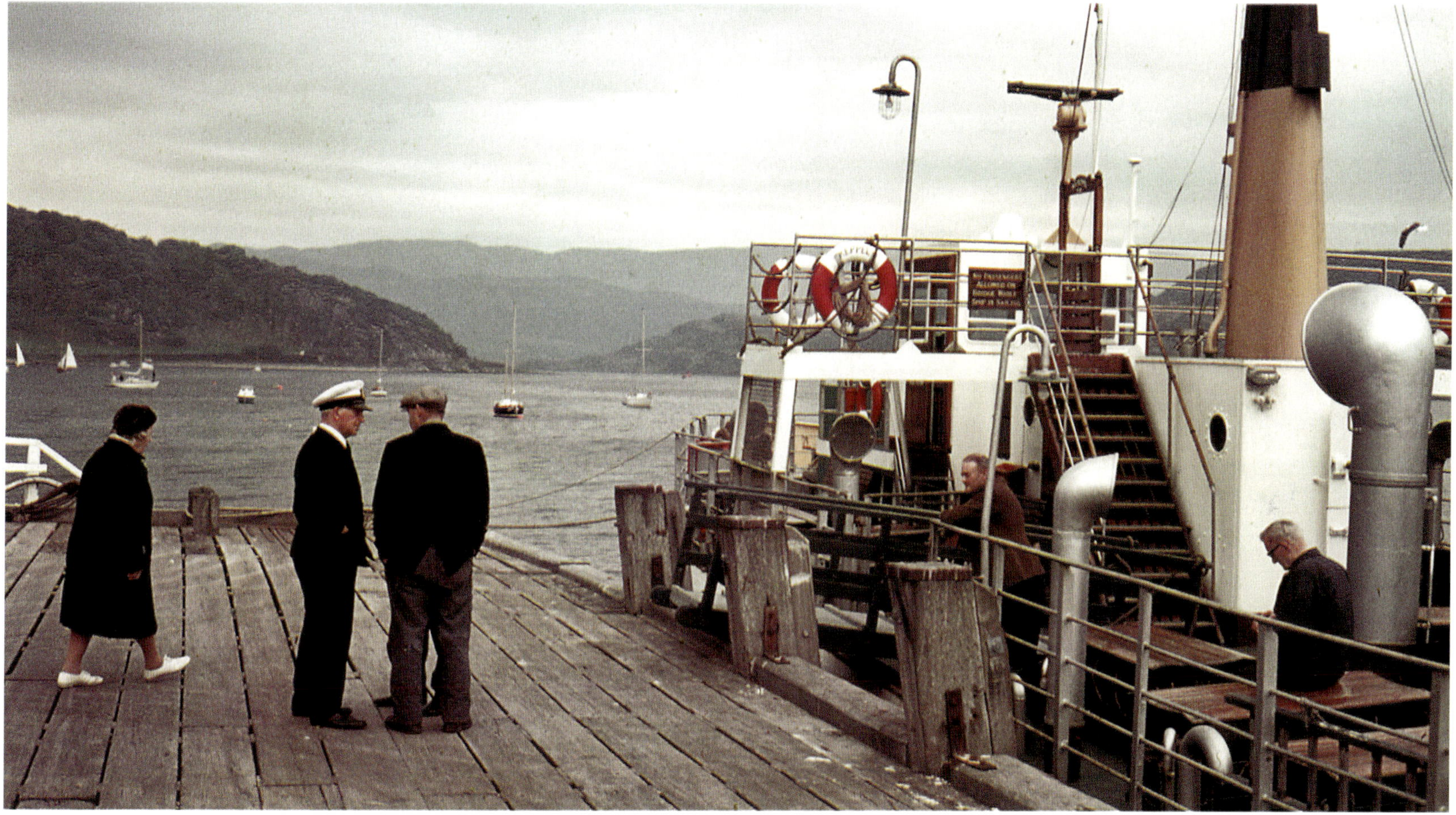

Tighnabruaich Pier on 26 May 1973: while the Largs-Millport ferry *Keppel* makes one of her rare visits to the Kyles, her skipper, Donald Macleod (in officer's cap), talks to a pier hand. One of three sister ships built in 1961 for the Tilbury-Gravesend ferry on the Thames, she was originally named *Rose*. After *Talisman* was withdrawn in 1966, the Caledonian Steam Packet Company needed a small but spacious ferry to operate alongside a 'Maid' at Millport. *Rose* was brought north, modified for Clyde service and renamed. As *Keppel* she built a reputation for slowness, sturdiness and manoeuvrability: she was the first Clyde vessel with a Voith Schneider propeller, making it possible to 'turn on a sixpence' – a trick Macleod used to full advantage when berthing at piers. From 1986 she served as Caledonian MacBrayne's cruise boat, in which capacity she began to visit the Kyles of Bute more frequently. Sold to Malta in 1995, she still operates there, easily recognisable to Scottish holidaymakers who remember her from her Clyde years.

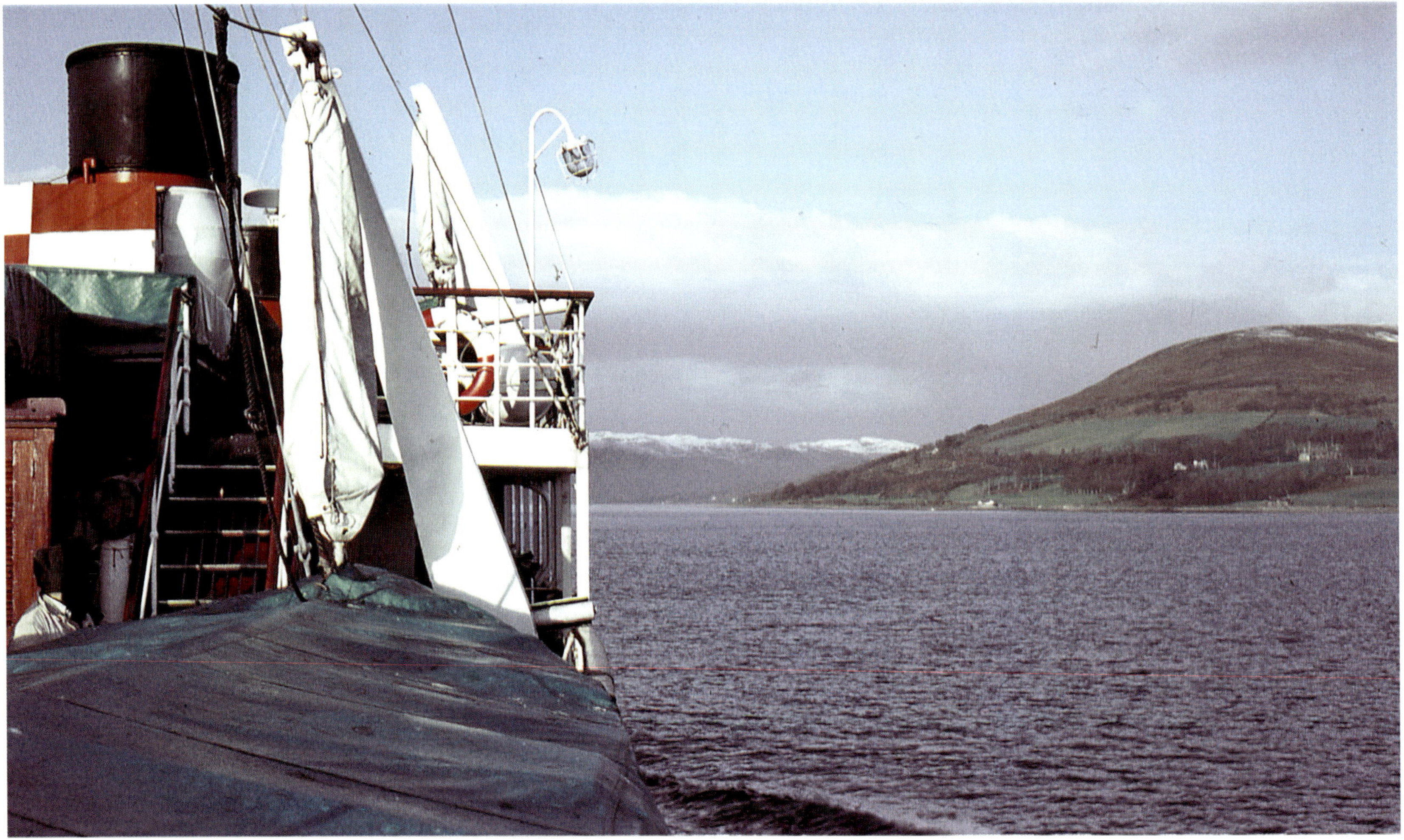

Lochfyne heads up the East Kyle on 2 January 1968 – a day of winter chill and brilliant sunshine, when the scenery must have been every bit as captivating as on a summer's day, if not more so. Until Easter 1970 it was possible to sail through the Kyles of Bute to Loch Fyne every working day of the year, thanks to David MacBrayne Ltd's Royal Mail service. Built in 1931 by Denny of Dumbarton, *Lochfyne* was a pioneering diesel-electric passenger vessel, renowned for her vibration. She served on the Tarbert and Ardrishaig service every winter in peacetime, and year-round after *Saint Columba*'s withdrawal in 1958.

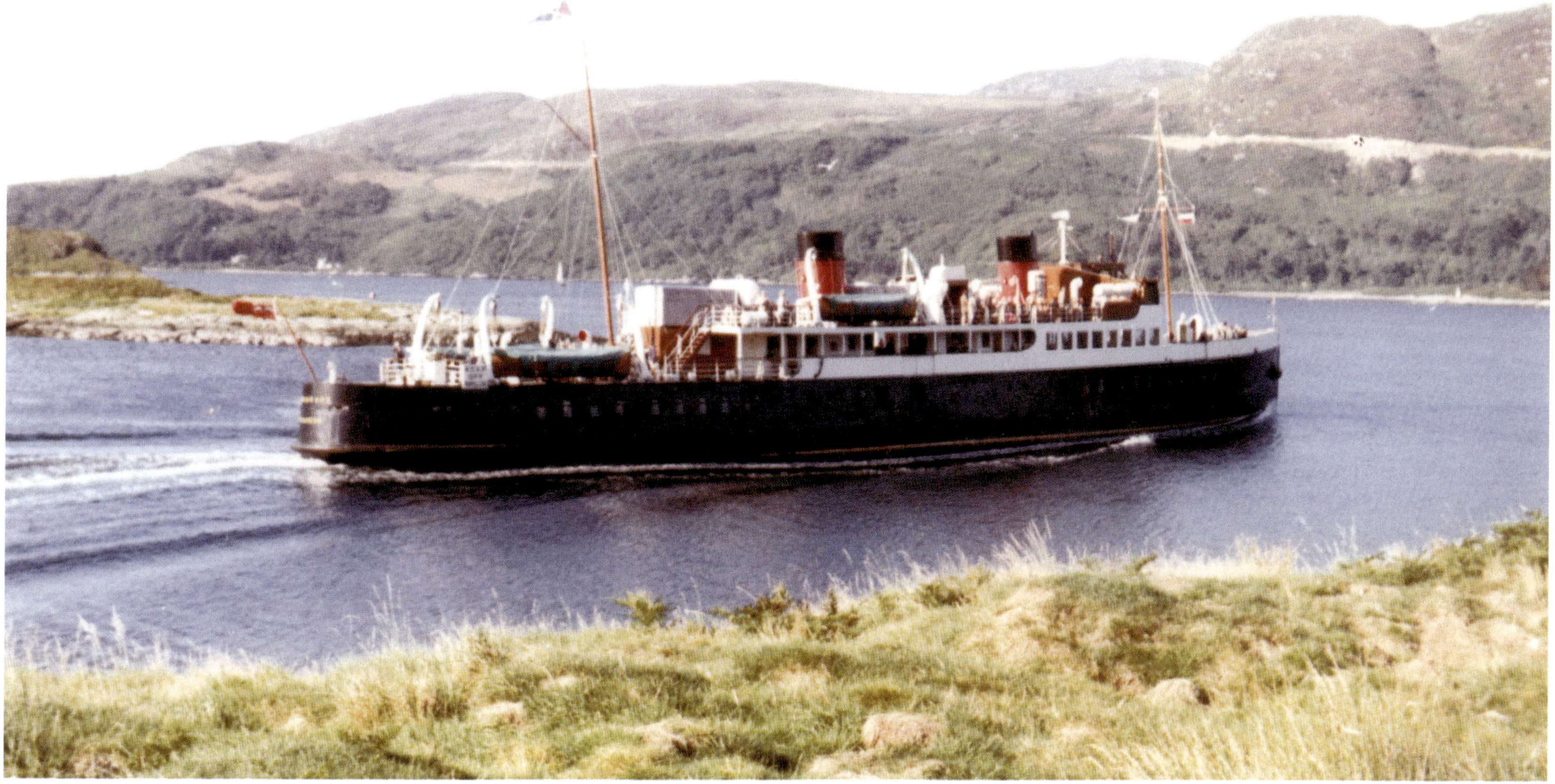

This photo of *Lochfyne* in the Narrows was taken on 15 September 1969, two weeks before her withdrawal from service. The photographer was Jim Aikman Smith, an idiosyncratic steamer enthusiast who used his own inflatable dinghy to cross to one of the islands in order to get a close-up. The distinctive MacBrayne flag flies from the aft mast, and construction of the 'new road' to Tighnabruaich is underway in the background. *Lochfyne* lacked the conventional beauty of the Clyde's railway-owned steamers, but as soon as you stepped aboard you could not fail to notice the distinctive atmosphere, recognisable on most MacBrayne boats – an atmosphere created by the highland accents and pillbox hats of the crew, and the sense of pride and dedication they took in their ship's time-served role as Royal Mail steamer.

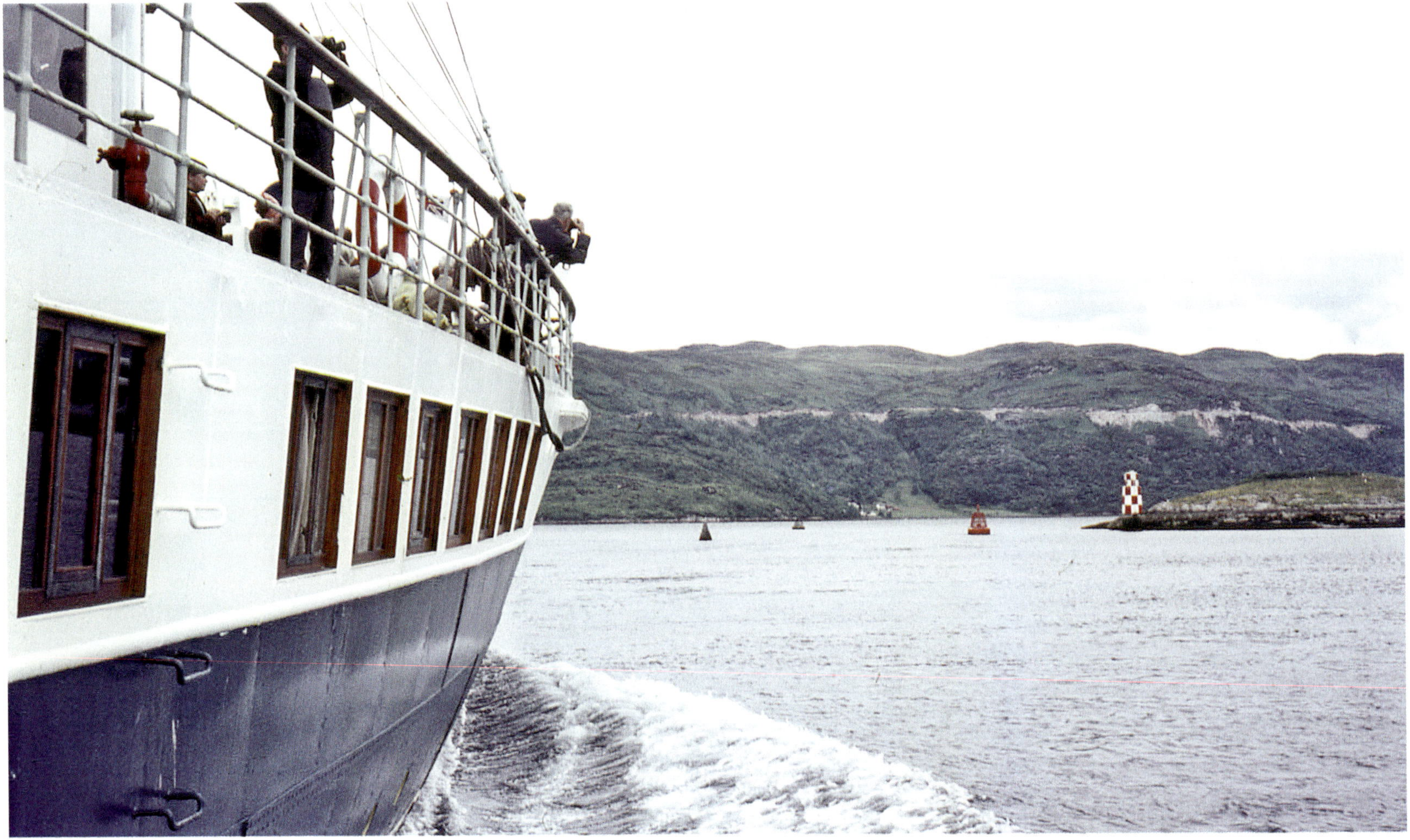

Caledonia's approach to the Narrows in 1969, seen from her starboard sponson (the section of the hull housing the paddle-boxes), illustrates how little room for error the pilot had when steering the ship through. The landscape in the background is of equal interest. It shows a scar running along the hillside – the beginnings of what is still known, 50 years later, as 'the new road'. At the time many decried it as a blot on the beautiful Kyles landscape, but the A8003 revolutionised Tighnabruaich's links with the outside world and provides a spectacular vantage point for tourists wanting to view the Kyles in all their glory. Today the road is barely visible from the water.

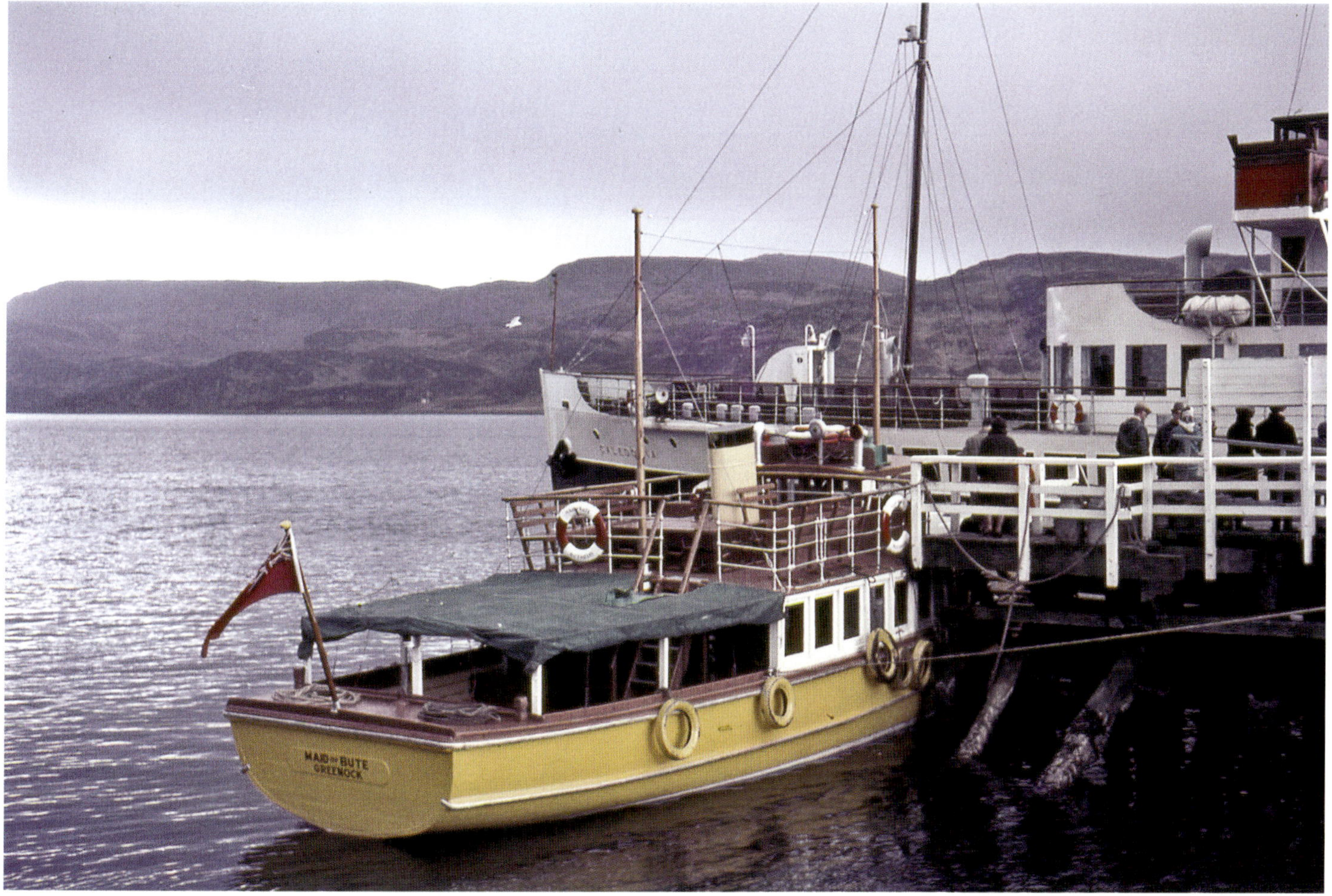

The beach at Tighnabruaich shelves suddenly, making it possible at low tide to approach the edge of the pier on foot from the shore and feel you are almost touching the vessel berthed alongside. On 20 April 1968 the tide was high enough for *Maid of Bute* to tie up at the side without any risk of her hitting the seabed or brushing against the forward section of *Caledonia*. Built at Fraserburgh in 1938 and based at Rothesay's Inner Harbour, *Maid of Bute* was a jolly little craft with a toy funnel and a decent turn of speed. In the post-war era she ran excursions independently of the railway-owned Clyde steamer fleet, making almost daily visits to the Kyles of Bute. She was sold to Fort William in 1973 and later the Firth of Forth and the Thames, before moving in 1998 to Falmouth in Devon and St Mawes in Cornwall.

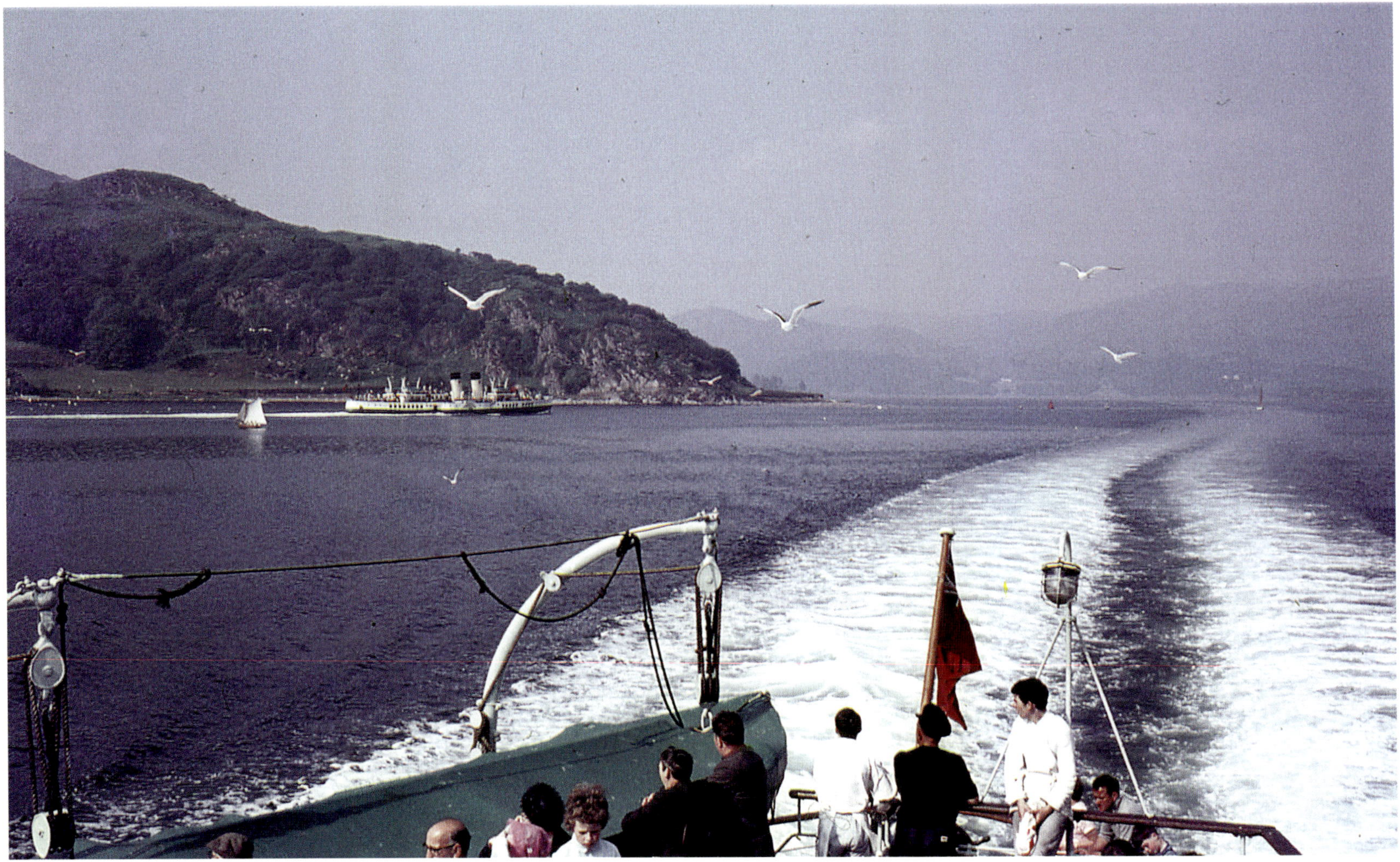

Summer idyll in 1968: it is Sunday 16 June, and *Waverley* is heading past the spit at Rhubaan on her way back to Rothesay, Largs and Millport, leaving Tighnabruaich Pier free for *Caledonia,* which is on a similar afternoon excursion from Craigendoran. When you see the number of people crowding the decks in steamer photographs of the 1960s, you wonder why it is that, half a century later, the River Clyde is so quiet and the Firth so bereft of excursion ships. The answer lies in the motor car, the foreign holiday, changing habits – and yes, maybe the weather.

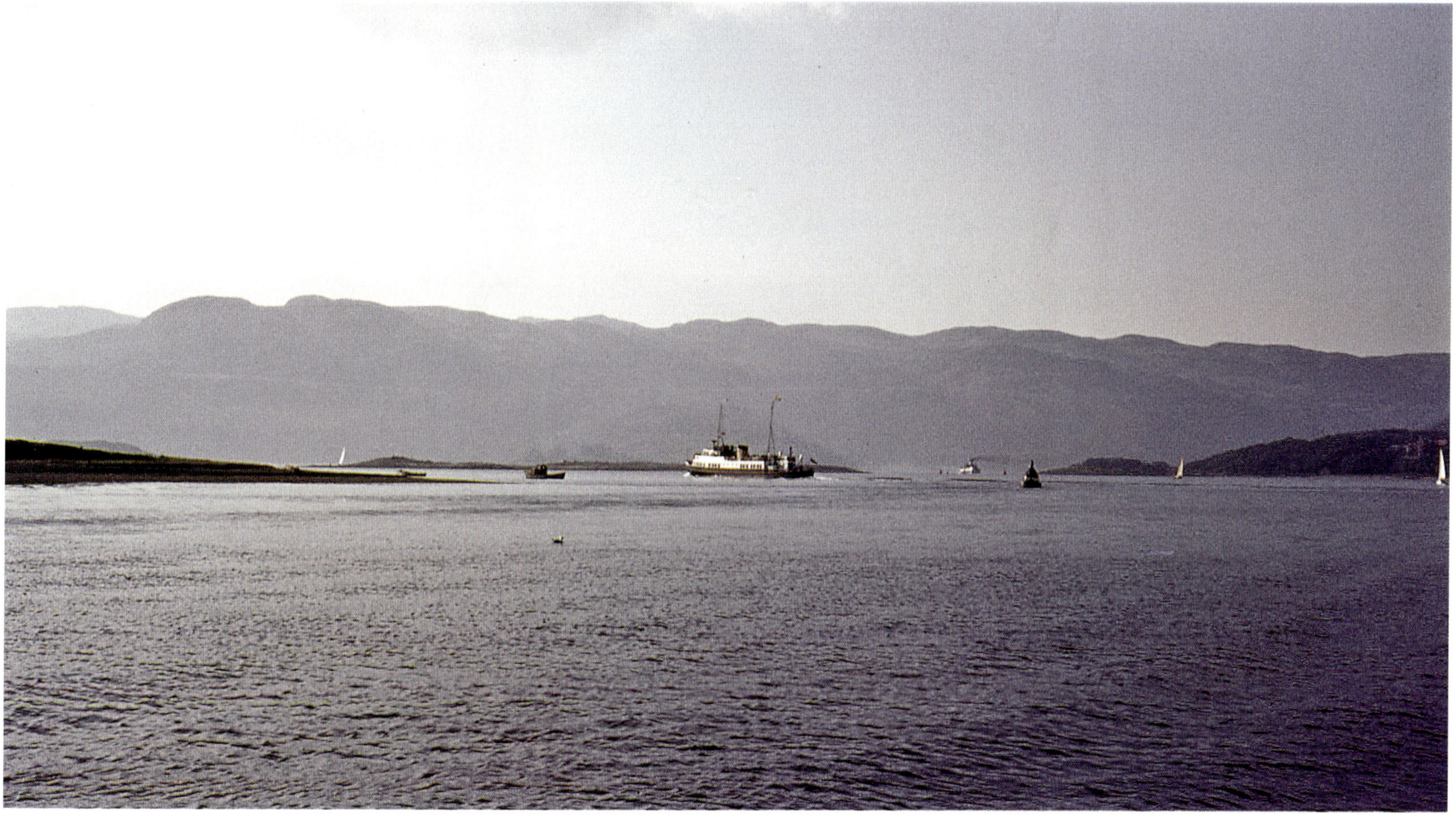

Daily excursion traffic through the Kyles continued in summer until the 1970s, but there are few surviving photographs of steamers meeting at the Narrows, as pictured here on Sunday 12 September 1971. In the foreground *Maid of Skelmorlie*, on the afternoon Craigendoran-Tighnabruaich excursion, is diverting to port (left hand side) in the direction of the dogleg channel. The purpose is not only to give *Waverley*, on the Round Bute cruise, a clear passage through the main channel, but also to allow *Maid of Cumbrae*, just out of sight, to follow *Waverley* through on her return sailing from Tighnabruaich to Millport. The 'Maids' were a quartet of passenger vessels that introduced diesel engines to the railway-owned Clyde fleet in 1953. The 1970s car ferry revolution made them redundant. *Maid of Argyll*, *Maid of Ashton* and *Maid of Skelmorlie* left the Clyde in the early 1970s. *Maid of Cumbrae* had her accommodation modified for car-carrying in 1972 and was sold to Italy in 1978.

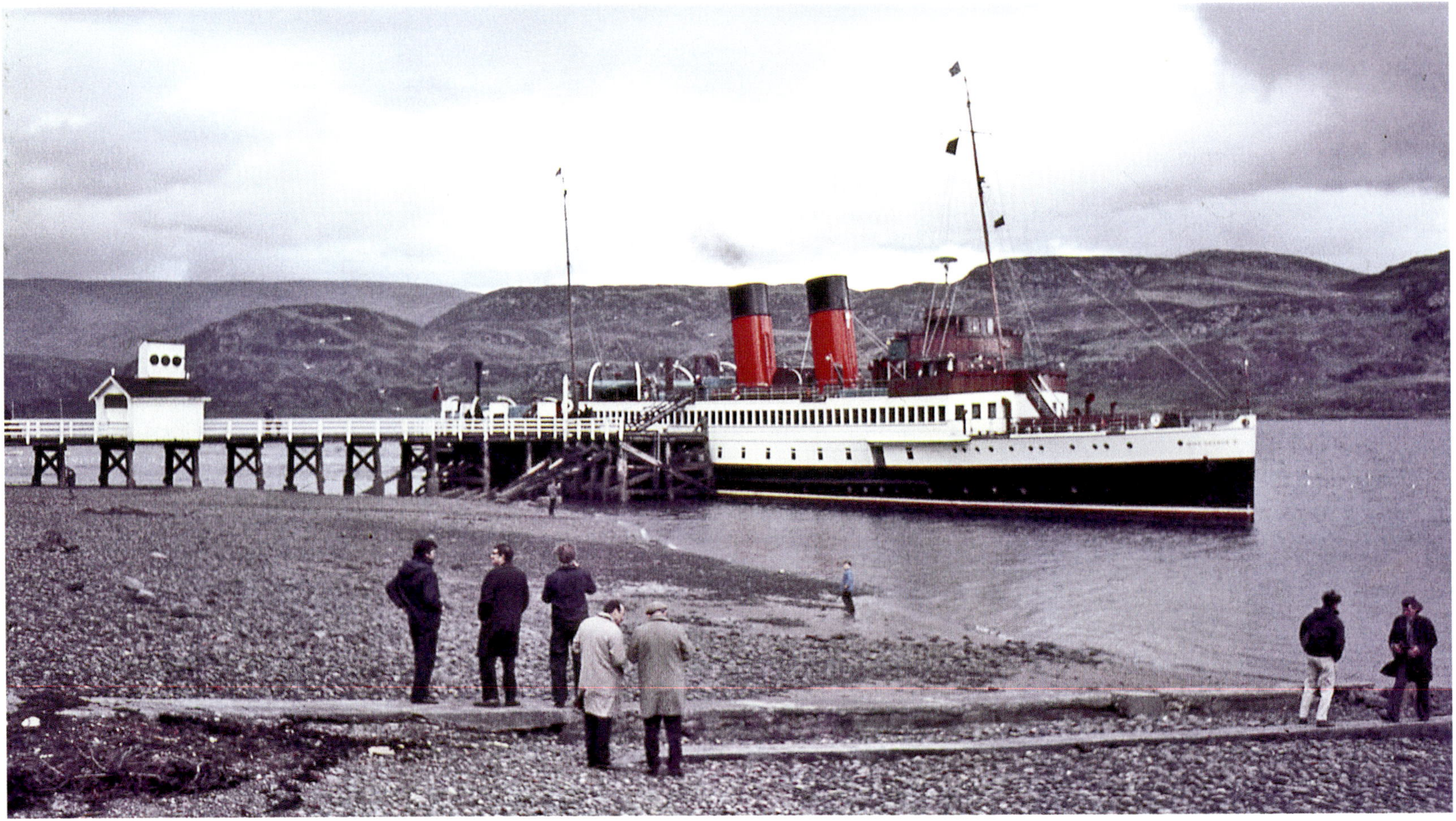

King George V was a revolutionary ship in her day. Built by Denny of Dumbarton in 1926 for Turbine Steamers' long-distance excursions to Campbeltown and Inveraray, she was the first Clyde steamer to be powered by high-pressure geared turbines, the first with an enclosed shelter deck and the first to have her dining saloon on the main deck, allowing passengers to view the passing scenery while eating. Sold to David MacBrayne Ltd late in 1935, she became the much loved Iona steamer, always returning to the Clyde for winter lay-up. In her last five years of service (1970-74) she gave a series of special excursions on the Clyde before heading for Oban for the summer. By this stage in her career *King George V* had achieved venerable status, and her sailings were snapped up by enthusiasts, who admired the immaculate way she was spruced up every spring. She is pictured at Tighnabruaich on 27 May 1971, when she was chartered by the Clyde River Steamer Club to sail round Bute from Gourock and Wemyss Bay.

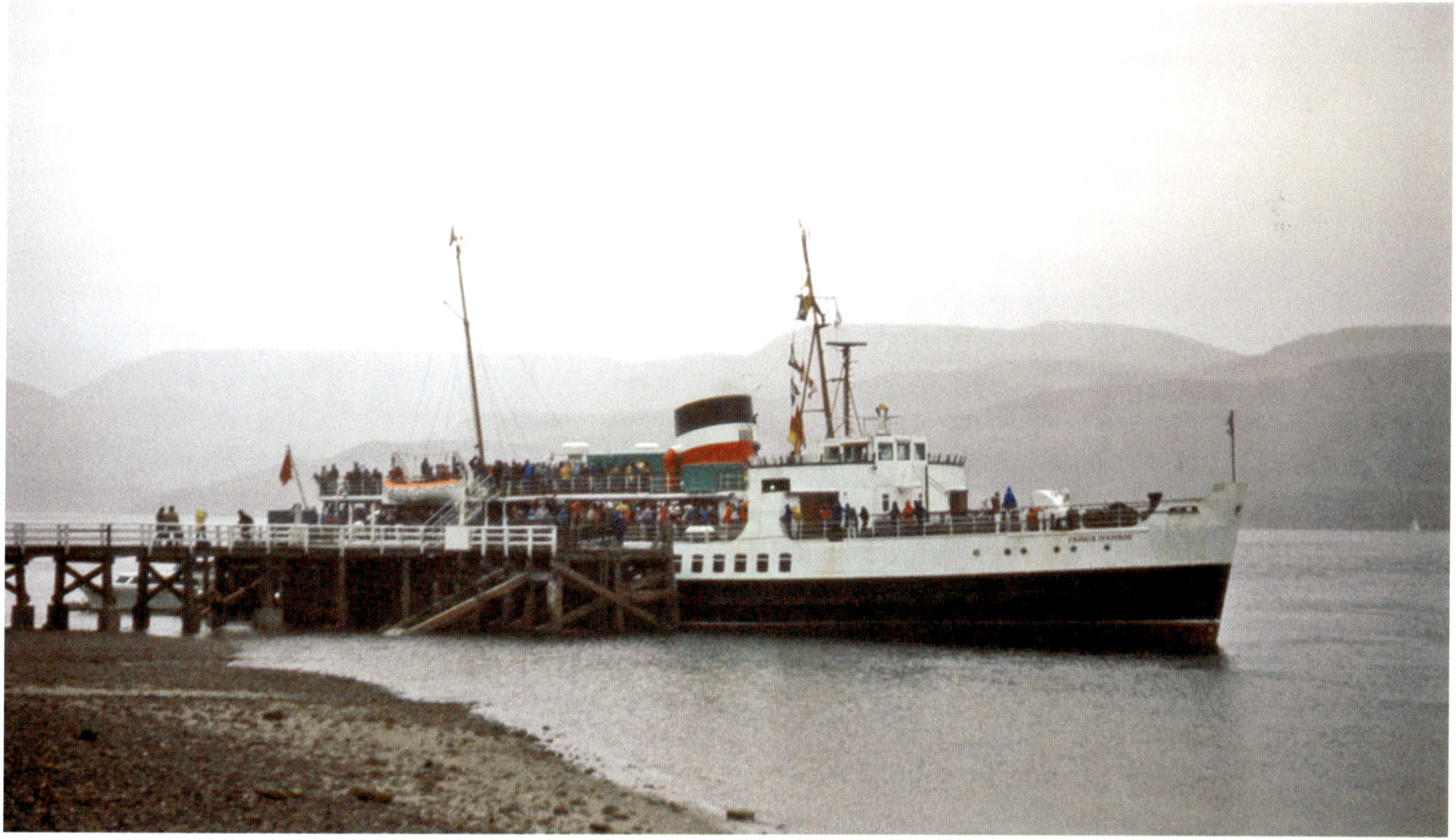

In 1981 the Clyde was presented, all too briefly, with a 'new' excursion steamer – the former Isle of Wight diesel ferry *Shanklin*. Built at Dumbarton in 1948, she had a useful career on the Portsmouth-Ryde run, before being bought in 1980 by the Firth of Clyde Steam Packet Company, an offshoot of the Waverley Steam Navigation Company. As a back-up for *Waverley* she seemed a good prospect: she was solidly built and had spacious decks. Repainted in WSN colours and renamed *Prince Ivanhoe*, she undertook a variety of sailings on the Bristol Channel and the Clyde in the early summer of 1981, and is pictured at Tighnabruaich on Saturday 16 June – a week before leaving the Clyde for good. On 3 August she struck a submerged object while cruising off the Gower Coast in South Wales, forcing the captain to run her ashore. All 490 passengers were safely landed but the vessel was a write-off.

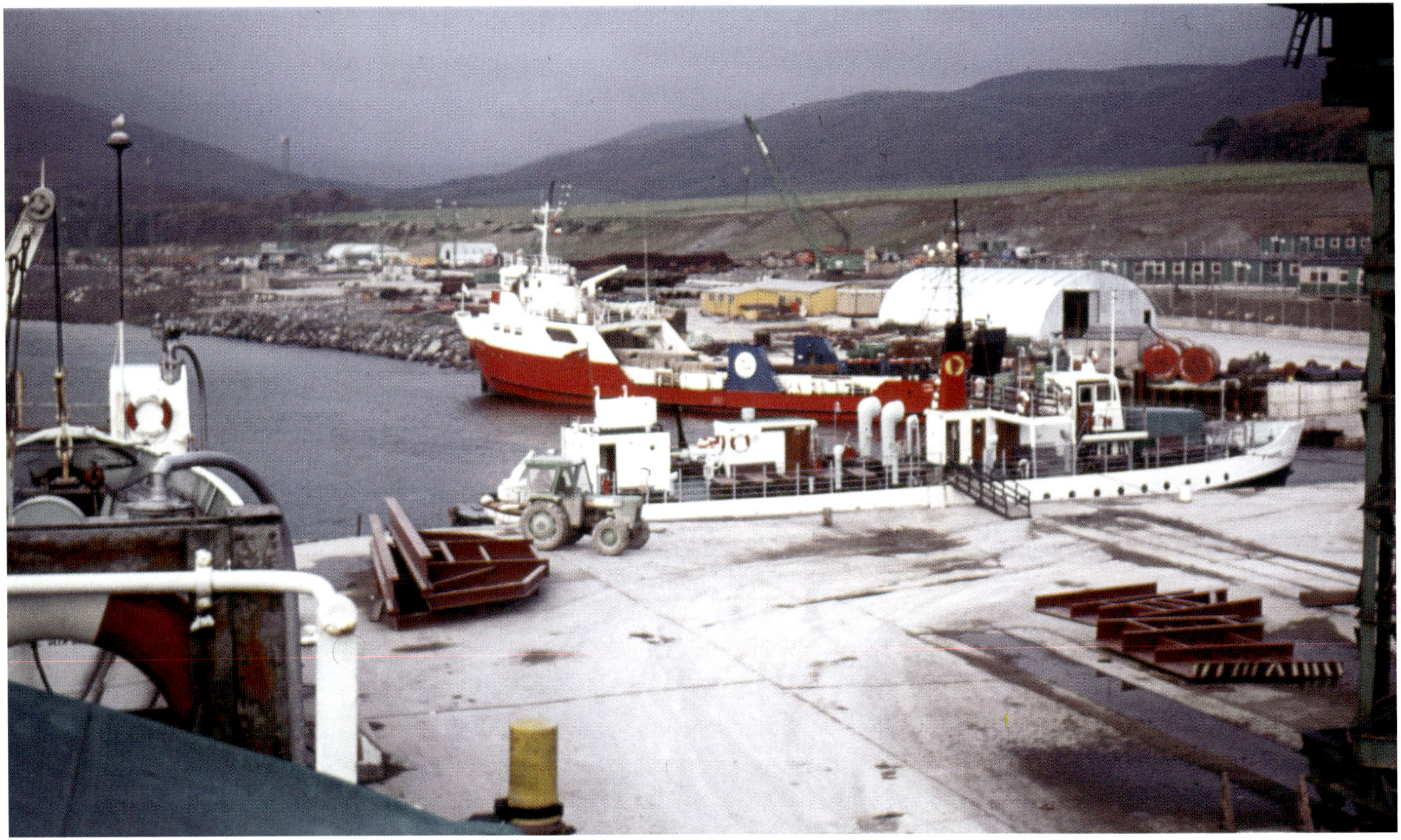

Sir Robert McAlpine's oil rig construction site at Ardyne, on the Cowal peninsula opposite the mouths of Loch Striven and the East Kyle, was a phenomenon of the mid 1970s. Initially workers were transported daily from Wemyss Bay via Innellan, but on 1 October 1974 the CalMac ferry *Bute* hanselled a new quay at Ardyne, and soon all manner of vessels were calling – including Western Ferries' red-hulled *Sound of Islay*, the Millport ferry *Keppel* (foreground) and the mighty *Glen Sannox*, from which this photo was taken in October 1975. By 1979, when *Waverley* called on a Paddle Steamer Preservation Society charter on 15 September (facing page), the oil workers had moved elsewhere and the place resembled a deserted salvage yard.

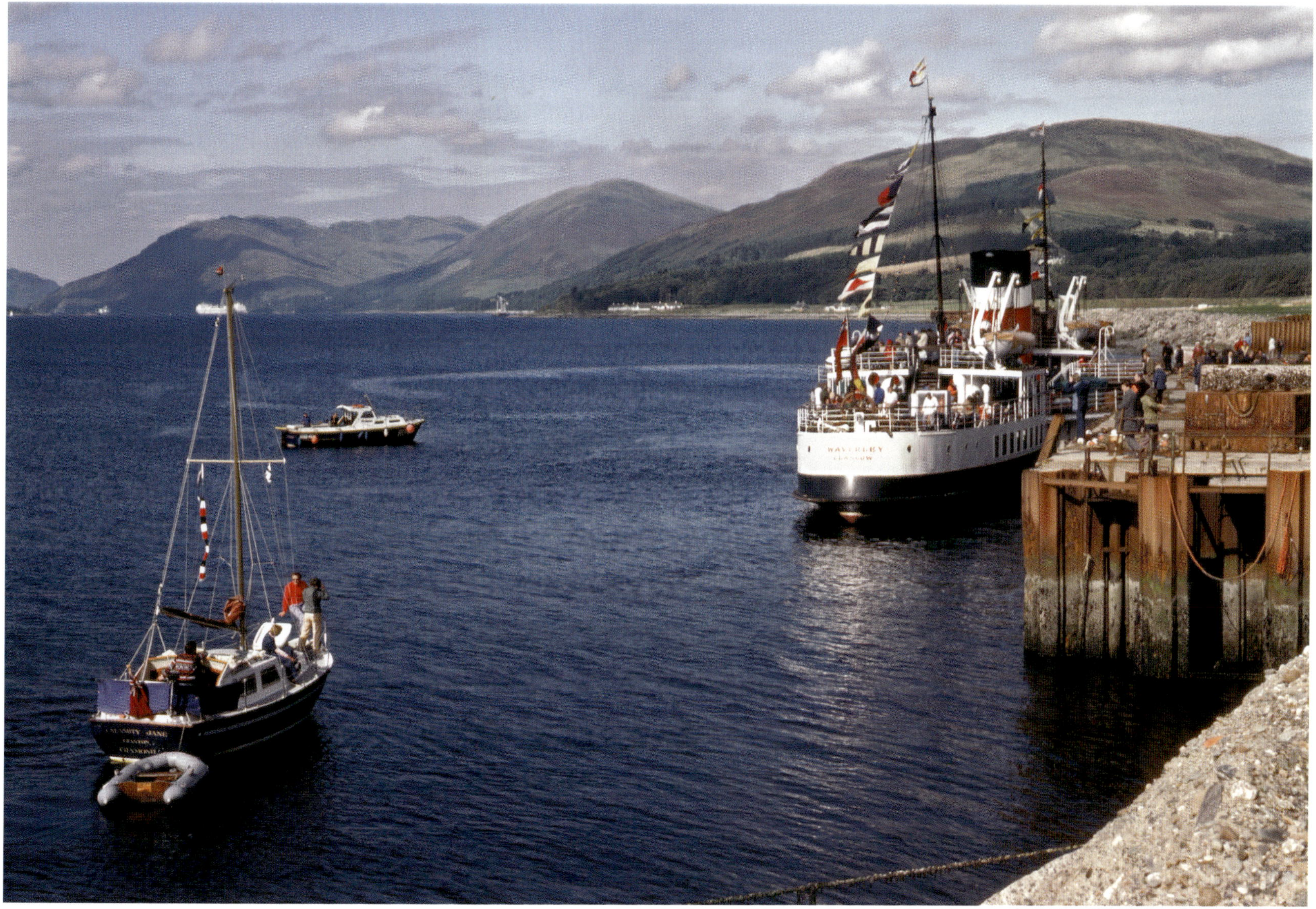
WAVERLEY

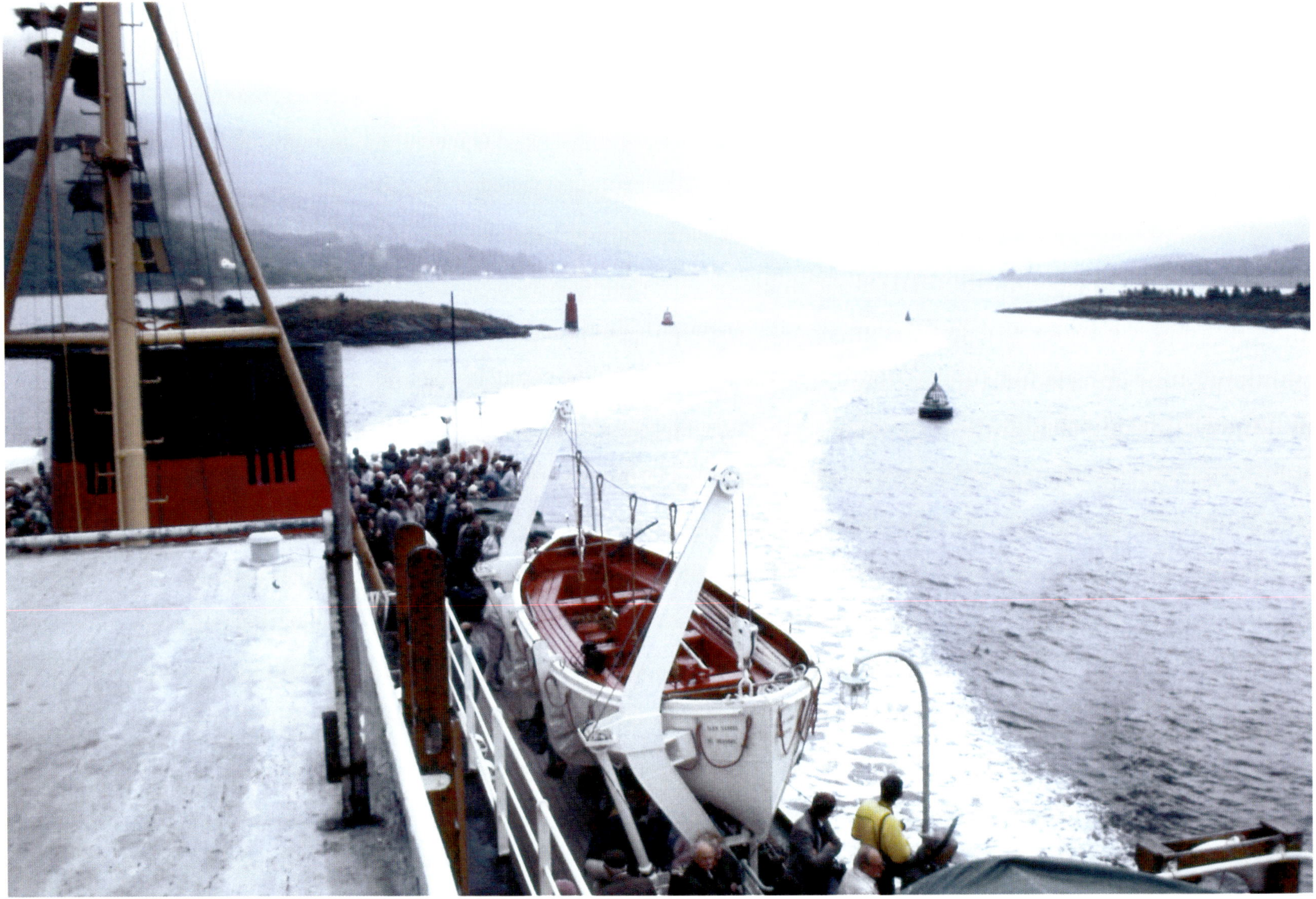

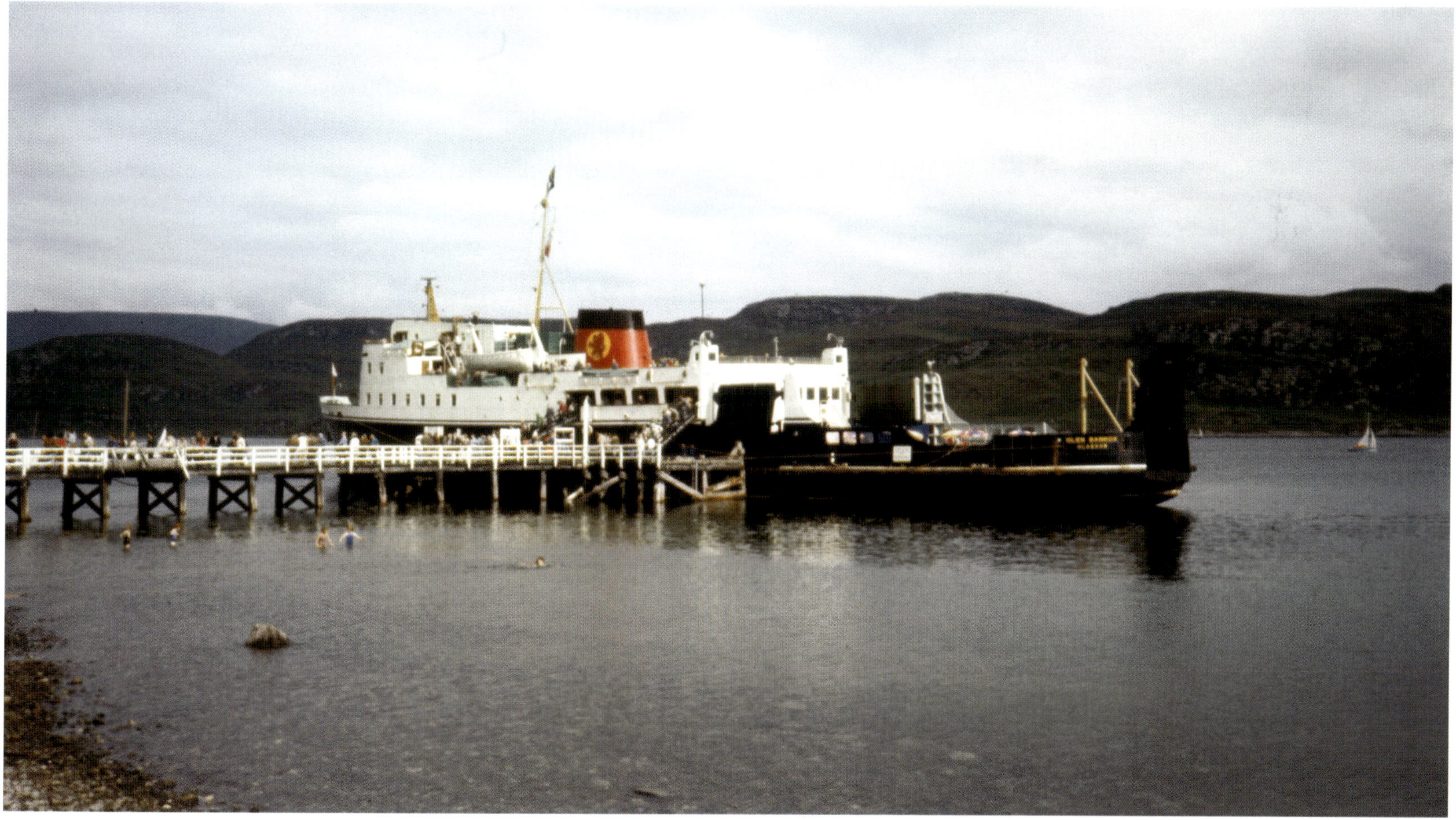

Facing page: in 1969, when the car ferry *Glen Sannox* first visited the Kyles of Bute, it seemed a miracle that such a beamy ship could fit through the Narrows. That occasion was a special charter, but in the late 1970s and early 1980s, reincarnated as CalMac's cruise boat, the 'Sannox' made the passage through the Narrows regularly. Given her size, it required expert shiphandling – as can be gauged from this photograph taken from her 'monkey island' (the deck above the wheelhouse). *Above*: at Tighnabruaich, *Glen Sannox* dwarfed the little pier to such an extent that the gangway took on an unusually steep gradient – but the time-honoured pleasures of a call there were just the same. Described as 'a tenement on a bathtub' when she came out on the Arran run in 1957, *Glen Sannox* ended up as one of CalMac's most popular and versatile vessels, renowned for her speed and spaciousness. She was sold to the Red Sea in 1989.

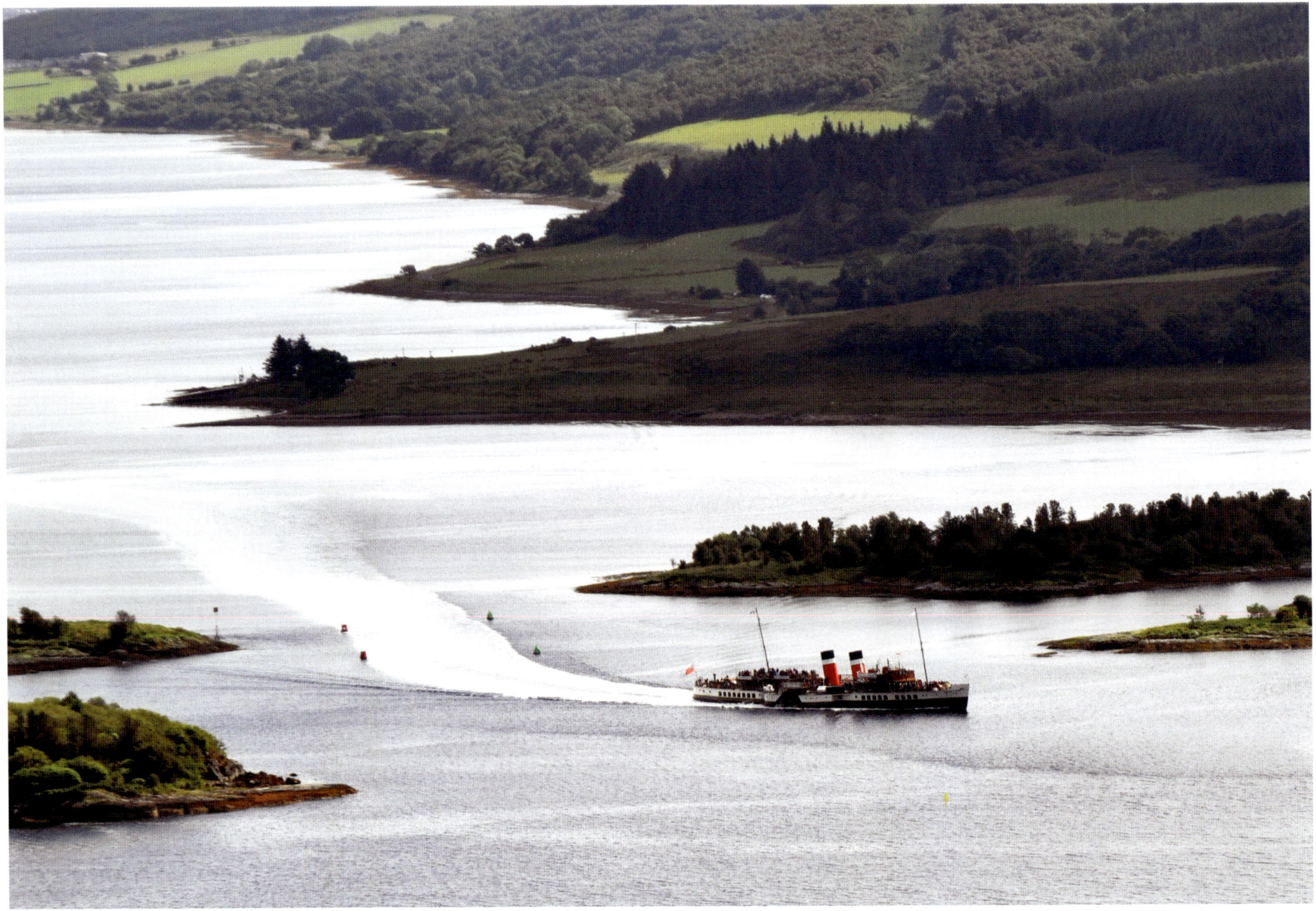

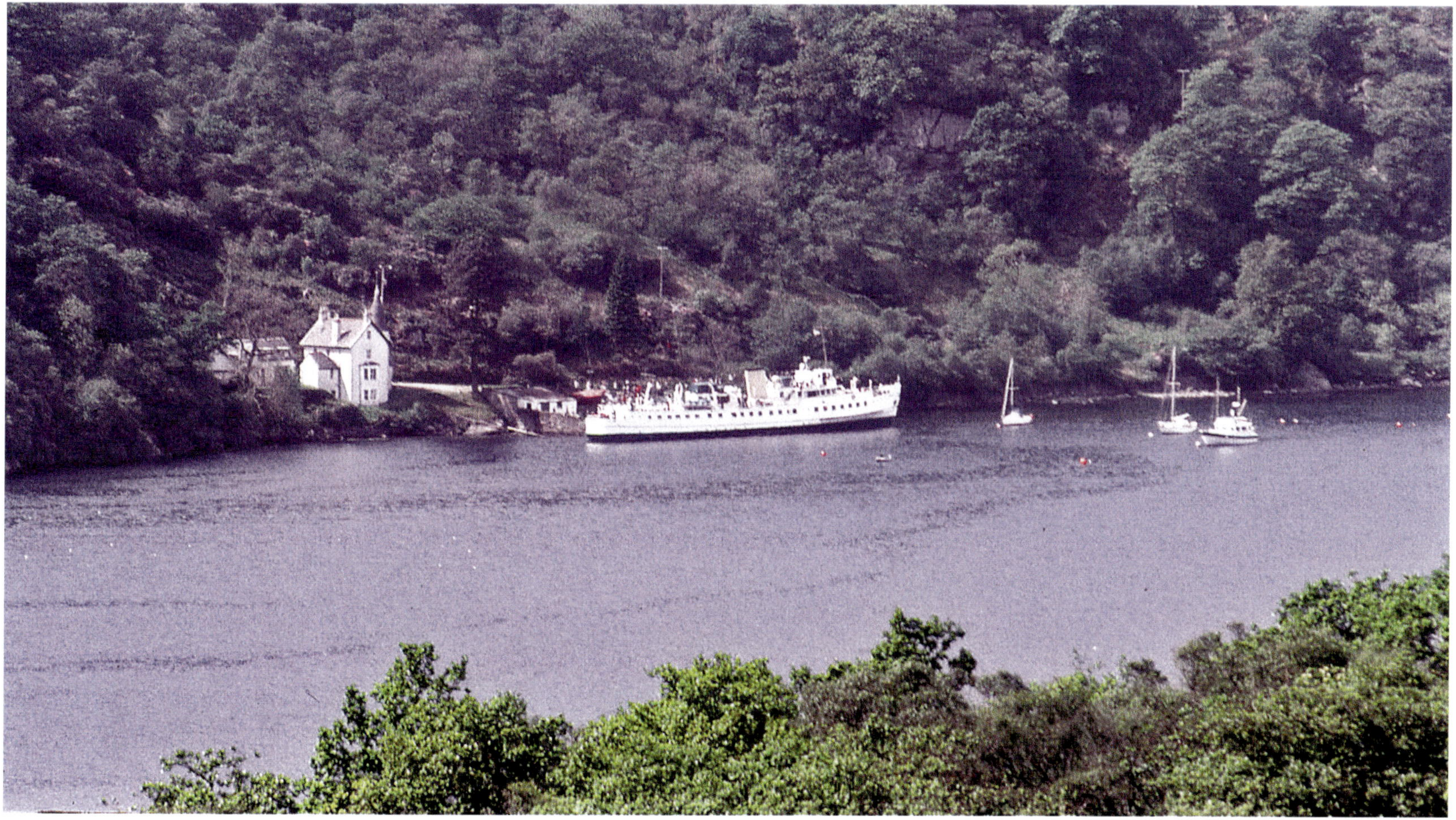

Facing page: the number of excursion steamers passing through the Kyles of Bute may have dwindled to one, but *Waverley* still needs to steer a delicate course between all manner of yachts and pleasure craft, not all of whom can be guaranteed to follow the rules of the sea. This panorama, showing the paddler on course for Tighnabruaich, was taken from one of the viewing points on 'the new road' and provides a graphic overview of the Narrows, with the dogleg channel on the right. *Above*: Ormidale looks as secluded as it ever was, with *Balmoral* lying peacefully at the pier on 26 May 1990. Built at Cowes in 1949 for the Southampton-Isle of Wight service, *Balmoral* was purchased by *Waverley*'s owners in 1989 as a back-up to the paddler, keeping alive the tradition of coastal cruising in parts of the British Isles that would not otherwise have the opportunity. Until recently she was a welcome visitor to the Clyde in the early or late season. Owned since 2014 by a Bristol-based charity, she has struggled to cover her costs, making her future uncertain.

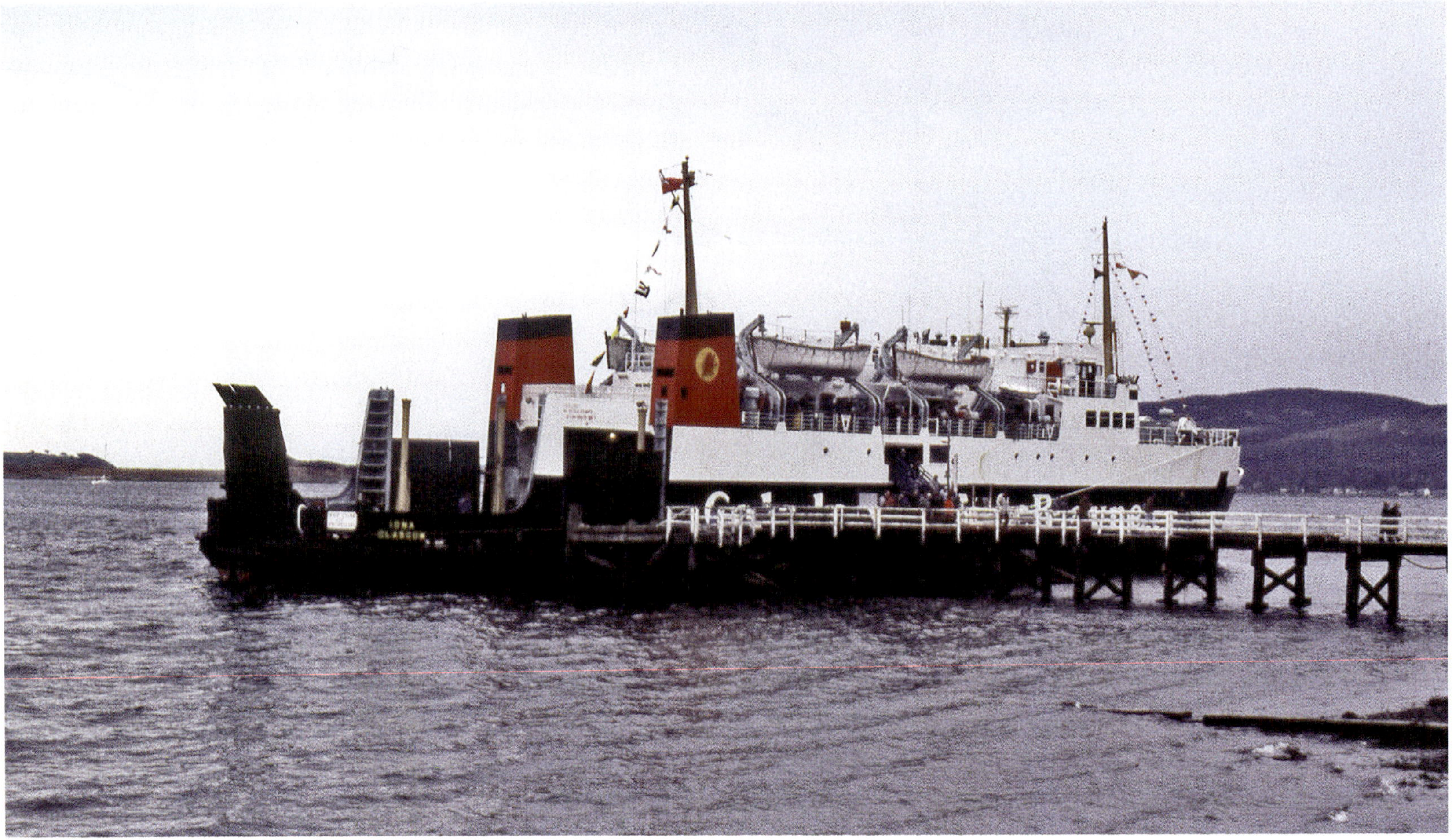

Apart from *Glen Sannox*, the biggest CalMac ferry to visit Tighnabruaich has been *Iona*. She called there on 3 April 1993 as part of a 'Walter Special' – the name given to a series of exotic cruises organised in the 1980s and 1990s by CalMac's Marketing Officer, Walter Bowie. That day *Iona* made four 'first calls' – at Wemyss Bay, Tarbert and Rothesay, in addition to the Kyles pier. By the end of her CalMac career in 1997 she had visited every pier in the network, a remarkable record that is unlikely to be beaten. Built by Ailsa of Troon in 1970, *Iona* was the first MacBrayne ferry to be designed for drive-through operation. After being sold by CalMac, she had a decade of service as *Pentalina B* on the Pentland Firth. She left UK waters in 2009 for Cape Verde, where she was wrecked in 2014.

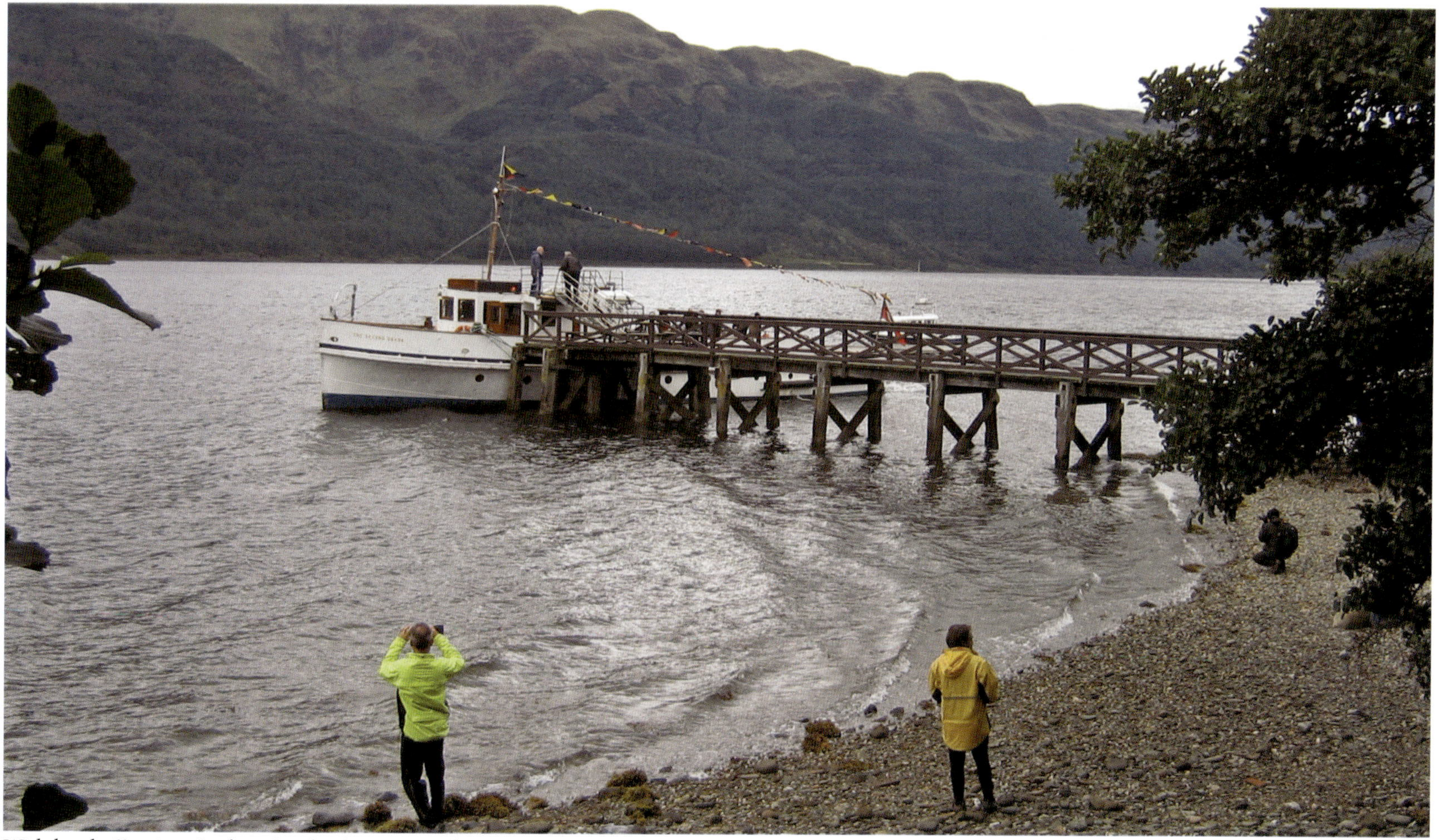

With her hull painted white for the first time in her long career, *The Second Snark* lies at Berry's Pier on 7 September 2013, during a charter by the Coastal Cruising Association. This was the second time 'the Snark' had visited the remote Loch Striven pier since it was rebuilt in the late 1990s, using timbers from the dismantled pier at Innellan. Built by Denny of Dumbarton in 1938 as a shipyard tender, *The Second Snark* led a remarkably varied life on the east and west coasts of Scotland. Latterly owned by Clyde Marine, the Greenock-based ferry and tug operator, she was able to visit places where larger vessels could not venture: on at least one occasion she made the passage through the narrow harbour at Glen Caladh at the entrance to Loch Riddon. In 2017 she was sold to an American businessman.

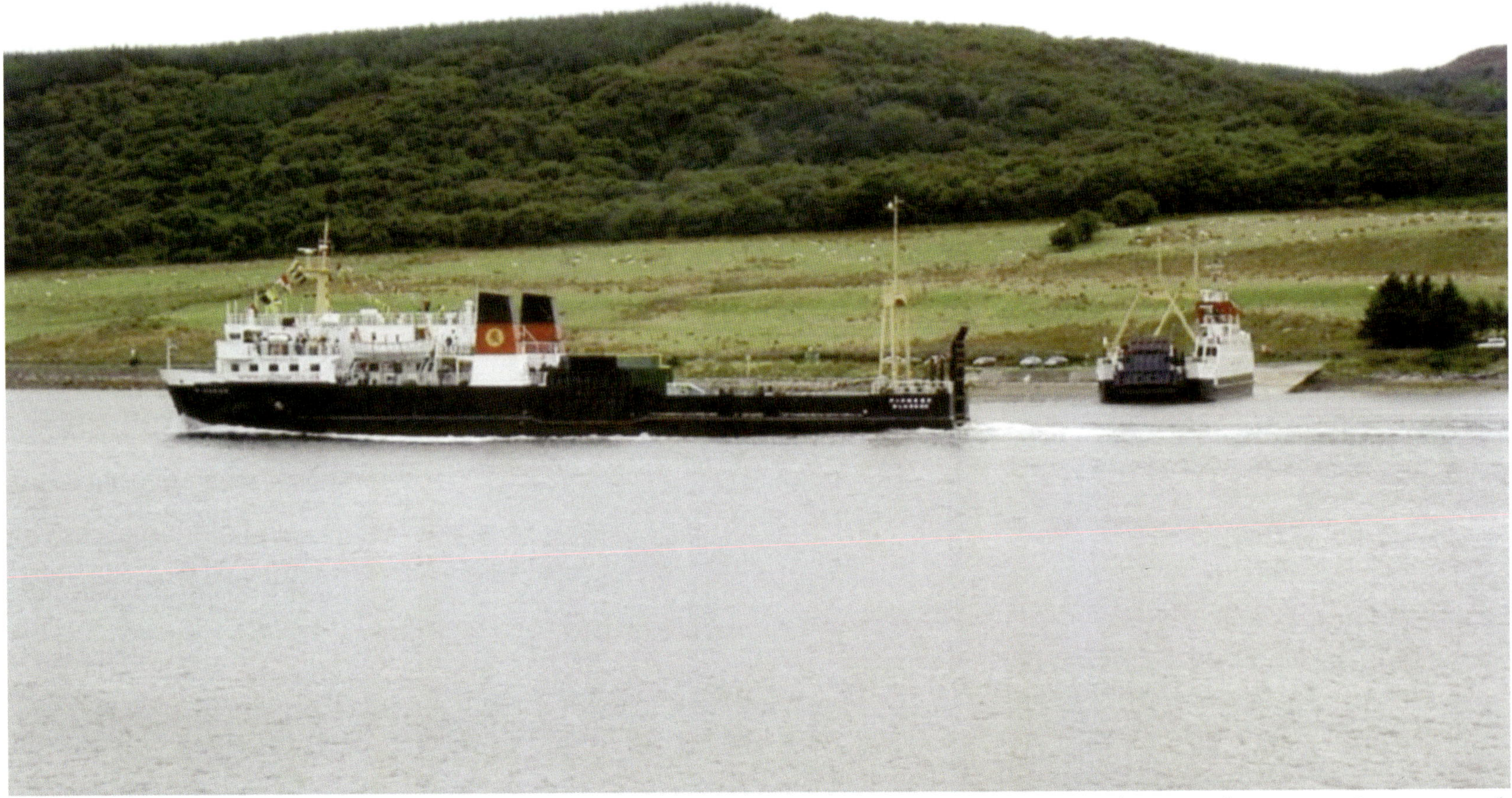

Pioneer heads down the East Kyle, passing *Loch Dunvegan* at Rhubodach. Designed for the Islay run *Pioneer* made her debut there in 1974, but spent much of the 1980s and 1990s filling in gaps elsewhere – notably on the Clyde, where she gave cruises in addition to her bread-and-butter work on the Dunoon, Rothesay and Arran runs. One of her cruise destinations was Tarbert, taking her regularly through the Kyles, and it was on a farewell excursion round Bute on 31 August 2003 that she last visited Tighnabruaich, followed by a final passage through the Narrows.

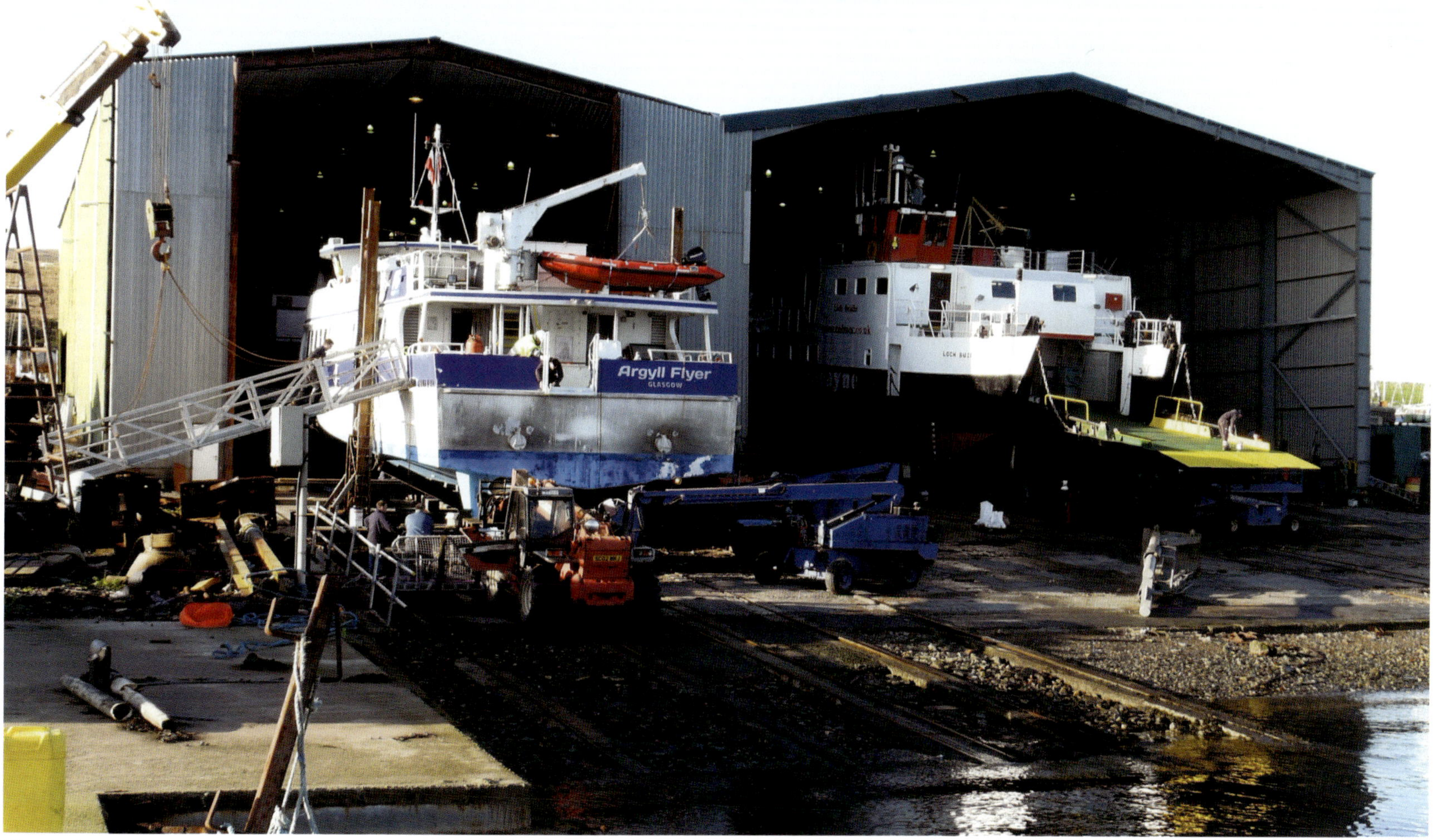

The Ardmaleish Boat Building Company at Ardmaleish Point on Bute is a local landmark, passed by every craft entering the East Kyle. In the post-war era the yard had a tumbledown appearance, but over the past quarter-century it has raised its game, and is now the repair yard used by operators of small ferries on the west of Scotland. The Gourock-Dunoon passenger ferry *Argyll Flyer* (left) and the Iona ferry *Loch Buie* are pictured undergoing annual overhaul on 22 November 2011. The yard now has three slips capable of taking ships of up to 500 tons, and covered sheds for vessels up to 240 feet long.

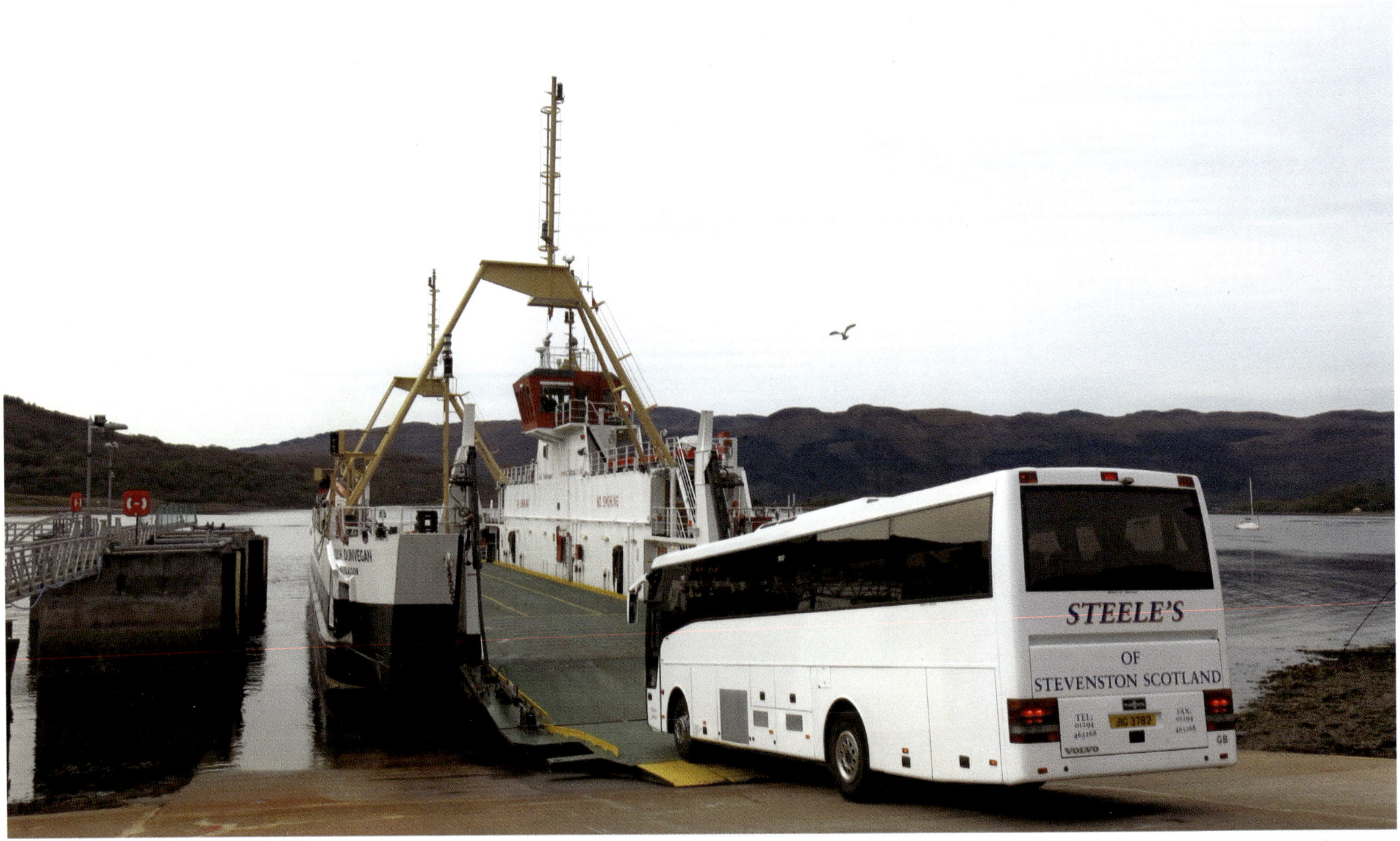

Since 1999 the Colintraive-Rhubodach connection has been maintained by *Loch Dunvegan*. Built in 1991 by Fergusons of Port Glasgow for the Skye crossing at Kyle of Lochalsh, she was made redundant by the opening of the Skye bridge only four years later. After a period of lay-up and uncertainty, she found a new lease of life in the East Kyle, where she greatly increased capacity on the crossing, her success leading to the construction of a special overnight berth and new ramps. While catering for Rothesay-Dunoon commuter traffic, she also provides an increasingly popular 'ferry hopper' link for bikers and tourists travelling from Wemyss Bay via Bute and Loch Fyneside to Kintyre.